around WASHINGTON, D.C. with KIDS

Credits
Writer: Kathryn McKay

Editors: Susan MacCallum-Whitcomb and Maria Hart
Editorial Production: Elyse Rozelle
Production Manager: Angela L. McLean

Design: Fabrizio La Rocca, *creative director*;
Tigist Getachew, *designer*
Cover Art and Design: Jessie Hartland
Flip Art and Illustration: Rico Lins, Keren Ora Admoni/
Rico Lins Studio

About the Writer
Writer Kathryn McKay covers a lot of ground, but her favorite place to write about is her hometown, Washington, D.C. She travels frequently with her two children and their nine cousins.

Seventh Edition
ISBN: 978-0-89141-974-7
ISSN: 1526-1980

Important Tip
Although all prices, opening times, and other details in this book are based on information supplied to us as of this writing, changes occur all the time in the travel world, and Fodor's cannot accept responsibility for facts that become outdated or for inadvertent errors or omissions. So always confirm information when it matters, especially if you're making a detour to visit a specific place.

Special Sales
This book is available at special discounts for bulk purchases for sales promotions or premiums. Special editions, including personalized covers, excerpts of existing books, and corporate imprints, can be created in large quantities for special needs. For more information, write to Special Markets/Premium Sales, 1745 Broadway, MD 3-1, New York, NY 10019, or email specialmarkets@randomhouse.com.

PRINTED IN THE UNITED STATES OF AMERICA
10 9 8 7 6 5 4 3 2 1

FUN TIMES A TO Z

BEST BETS

BEST IN TOWN
International Spy Museum, **51**
Mount Vernon, **44**
National Air and Space Museum, **42**
National Museum of American History, **32**
National Zoo, **25**

BEST OUTDOORS
Wheaton Regional Park (gardens and nature center), **3**

WACKIEST
D.C. Ducks, **60**

GROSSEST
National Museum of Health and Medicine, **30**

COLDEST
National Harbor's ICE!, **34**

BEST CULTURAL ACTIVITY
National Gallery of Art and Sculpture Garden, **36**

BEST MUSEUM
National Museum of Natural History, **29**

SOMETHING FOR EVERYONE

ART ATTACK
Corcoran Gallery of Art, **62**
Hirshhorn Museum and Sculpture Garden, **52**
National Gallery of Art and Sculpture
Garden, **36**
National Museum of African Art, **33**
National Museum of Women in the Arts, **27**
Phillips Collection, **21**
Sackler Gallery/Freer Gallery of Art, **17**
Smithsonian American Art Museum and the
National Portrait Gallery, **15**

CULTURE CLUB
National Museum of African Art, **33**
Sackler Gallery/Freer Gallery of Art, **17**

FARMS AND ANIMALS
Claude Moore Colonial Farm, **64**
National Aquarium, **40**
National Zoo, **25**
Oxon Cove Park, **23**
Patuxent National Wildlife Visitor Center, **22**
Rock Creek Park, **19**

GOOD SPORTS
Mystics Basketball, **43**
Washington Nationals, **4**
Wheaton Regional Park, **3**

HISTORIC HOUSES
Frederick Douglass National Historic Site, **56**
Glen Echo Park, **55**
Mount Vernon, **44**
Sully Historic Site, **14**
White House, **2**

LOST IN SPACE
College Park Aviation Museum, **63**
Goddard Space Flight Visitor Center, **54**
National Air and Space Museum, **42**
National Air and Space Museum's
Steven F. Udvar-Hazy Center, **41**

ALL AROUND TOWN

GET READY, GET SET!

What child wouldn't be excited to touch a moon rock, tour the most famous house in the country, or see Dorothy's ruby slippers? Washington may seem like a place that's mainly for grown-ups and school trips. After all, running the government of a superpower is serious stuff. But the city of the White House and the Capitol is also home to the International Spy Museum, the National Museum of Natural History, and the National Zoo. History that appears dry and dusty in the classroom comes alive for children as they visit landmarks they've seen in movies and on TV, ride horses through the same park where presidents have ridden, and watch thousands of dollars roll off the presses at the Bureau of Engraving and Printing. A big plus in Washington is that most attractions are free.

GET PREPARED

You could just take the Metro to the Smithsonian stop, get off at the National Mall, and wander around. And you'd probably have fun.

Or you can prepare yourself and your children. Flip through this book. The first time, flip through fast, and check out Abe Lincoln and his admirers in the lower right corner. Next, take the time to read the listings, and use the directories in the back of the book to find just what you're looking for. Last but not least, bring this book with you as you explore. It'll help you get even more out of your visits.

Before you leave, call for information—especially if you go on a holiday, when Washington is generally very crowded. The hours listed in this book reflect usual operating times. Some places might stay open longer or close earlier on holidays; others may not open at all. Hours, of course, are subject to change. So are fees. For those sights that do charge admission, we list only the regular adult, student (with ID), and kids' prices; children under the ages specified are free. In addition, some discounts are offered for families or for visitors with a particular status or affiliation, so it never hurts to ask.

To find current kids' activities and events going on in and around the city, look in (or click on) the "Weekend" section of Friday's *Washington Post* and in *Washington Parent*, a monthly publication available free at libraries and many grocery stores.

GET AROUND

For train lovers, riding Washington's Metro (subway) system can be as thrilling as exploring your destination. But before you go, remember that getting into a public restroom at Metro stations requires a special request. Buy your pass at the Farecard machines, or better yet, let your kids put their math minds to work and put the money in the machines. The base fare is $1.70; the actual price you pay depends on the time of day and distance traveled. Children ages four and under ride free. But after you go through the turnstiles to enter, collect your kids' cards. You'll need them again to exit.

Each line of the Metrorail is color coded: red, orange, blue, green, and yellow. You can move from one line to another at transfer stations. As a precaution, be sure shoelaces are tied and scarves are tucked in before you ride Metro escalators, some of which are more than 200-feet long. If your children are afraid of heights or you have a little one in a stroller, take the elevators. All the stations have them, though about a third of them are across the street from Metro entrances.

If, on the other hand, you decide to navigate behind the wheel, it's relatively easy to get your bearings in this diamond-shaped city. With the Capitol as its hub,

Washington is composed of four quadrants—Northwest (NW), Northeast (NE), Southwest (SW), and Southeast (SE)—divided by North, South, and East Capitol streets and, on the west side of the Capitol, by the National Mall instead of a street. Within each of these quadrants, the roads running north and south are numbered, and east to west roads are named after letters of the alphabet. (You won't find an A or B street because A Street became the Mall and East Capitol Street, and B Street was renamed Constitution Avenue to the north and Independence Avenue to the south.) After the lettered streets come longer street names in alphabetical order, and the alphabetical lineup repeats itself until the Maryland and Virginia borders. Add to the mix a number of diagonal avenues named for states, the most prominent being Massachusetts, Connecticut, and Pennsylvania avenues. Traffic circles and one-way streets can be confusing for adults but fun for kids, who can look for the statues and fountains in the centers of the circles.

Around the outskirts, the Capital beltway girds Washington like—you guessed it—a big belt. If you do go downtown, keep in mind that parking may be limited and expensive, particularly during the week. For most suburban sights, parking is free and plentiful.

GET ORIENTED

When you arrive at a sight, be prepared to walk through metal detectors and open your bags for security personnel. Visit the information desk for maps and brochures, and inquire about children's programs. Also, show your kids how to recognize staff or security people, and designate a time and place—some visible landmark—to meet in case you become separated. It goes without saying that you should keep an eye on your children at all times, especially if they are small.

GET GOING

Finally, after you've planned and scheduled and traveled, have fun. And try to be as spontaneous as your children.

GET IN TOUCH

We'd love to hear from you. What did you and your children think about the places we recommend? Have you found other places we should include? Send us your ideas via email (c/o editorsfodors.com, specifying *Around Washington, D.C. with Kids* on the subject line) or snail mail (c/o Around Washington, D.C. with Kids, Fodor's Travel, 1745 Broadway, New York, NY 10019). In the meantime, get ready, get set, and go have a great time seeing Washington, D.C. with your kids!

—Kathryn McKay

A cemetery doesn't seem like a place for children, but this one—the most famous and most visited burial ground in the country—is different. Even cynical observers of Washington's politic scene may find a lump in their throat or a tear in their eye while here. There is certainly plenty to see.

At the Tomb of the Unknowns, where unidentified fallen service members are traditionally laid to rest, soldiers from the Army's 3rd U.S. Infantry Regiment (Old Guard) keep watch 24/7, regardless of weather. Each sentinel marches 21 steps (children can count them silently), clicks his or her heels, and faces the tomb for 21 seconds, symbolizing the 21-gun salute—all while carrying an M14 rifle weighing 10 pounds. The changing of the guard is a precise ceremony, held every half hour during the day from April through September and every hour the rest of the year. (At night, when the cemetery is closed, it's every two hours.)

Kids may also be interested in famous grave sites. More than 400,000 American war dead—and many notable citizens—are interred in these 624 acres. Even children who

MAKE THE MOST OF YOUR TIME You can reach Arlington on the Metro, by foot over Arlington Memorial Bridge (southwest of the Lincoln Memorial), or by car (there's a large parking lot by the visitor center on Memorial Dr.). ANC Tours by Martz Gray Line ($8.75 adults, $4.50 children 3–11; tel. 202/488–1012; www.anctours.com) has dedicated site tours that depart multiple times per day from the visitor center. The hop-on-hop-off Old Town Trolley (tel. 888/910–8687; www.oldtowntrolley.com) also has a stop that serves Arlington National Cemetery.

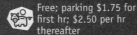
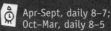
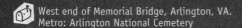

don't yet know the name John F. Kennedy may find the eternal flame at his final resting place fascinating. He's buried near two of his children, who died in infancy, and his wife, Jacqueline Bouvier Kennedy Onassis. President Kennedy's is the most visited grave in the country. If the flame is extinguished by rain, wind, or any other cause, a continuously flashing electric spark reignites it. Nearby, simple white crosses mark the plots of his brothers Robert and Edward (Teddy). William Howard Taft, 27th president and Supreme Court justice, also lies here, as do famous veterans Joe Louis (boxer), and Abner Doubleday (reputed inventor of baseball). Yet the sobering sea of marble headstones in Section 60 may have the greatest resonance today: This is where more than 800 men and women who died in Iraq and Afghanistan are buried.

If you like this sight, you may also like the Washington National Cathedral (#5).

EATS FOR KIDS

Plan carefully. No food or drink is allowed at the cemetery, but you can purchase and drink bottled water at the **Women in Military Service for America Memorial** near the entrance. There are also water fountains in the visitor center.

KEEP IN MIND Kids might think the Old Guard soldiers look cool in their sunglasses. The soldiers, however, aren't making a fashion statement—they're simply protecting their eyes from the sun's glare off the white marble of the tomb. More fun facts about the Cemetery are available via the *ANC Explorer*, an app that was introduced in 2012.

AUDUBON NATURALIST
SOCIETY'S WOODEND

Don't let bad weather keep the kids inside. In fact, no matter what it's like out, there'll be something interesting to see and do at this natural wonderland. Snow and mud make finding animal tracks easier as you play nature detective. On hot, humid days, crickets and cicadas form a chorus, while butterflies dance in wildflower meadows. On cool, crisp fall days, you can see varied leaf colors reflected in the large pond. But on any day, you'll hear the trill of birdsong because the Audubon Naturalist Society (ANS) has turned the grounds into a nature sanctuary.

A self-guided trail winds through this verdant 40-acre venue and around the local ANS's suburban Maryland headquarters. The estate is known as Woodend, as is the mansion, which was designed in the 1920s by Jefferson Memorial architect John Russell Pope. Allowing time to marvel at Mother Nature, you can complete the ¾-mile trail in about one hour. Parents of babies should use a carrier rather than a stroller, as most of the trail has wood chips. Along it, you'll see not only birdhouses and bird feeders, but also houses for flying squirrels.

KEEP IN MIND
The beauty and tranquillity of this sanctuary might be punctured from time to time by the sight of a Cooper's hawk making a meal out of a mourning dove, the remains of a mouse that an owl has discarded, or the roar of the Washington Beltway.

EATS FOR KIDS Pack a picnic for your adventure at nearby **Chevy Chase Supermarket** (8531 Connecticut Ave., tel. 301/656–5133), a neighborhood institution since 1958. Or, about 3 miles west in downtown Bethesda, nibble your way around the world at any of 180 restaurants. As its name implies, **Mama Lucia's** (4916 Elm St., tel. 301/907–3399) specializes in Italian dishes. Monday is pasta special night; on Tuesday, pizza prices are slashed. Fast, friendly service and red chili-pepper lights swooping across the ceiling make **California Tortilla** (4871 Cordell Ave., tel. 301/654–8226) a family favorite. For a dining guide call the Bethesda Urban Partnership at 301/215–6660.

For a break from the outdoors and the heat (the mansion is now air-conditioned), ask at the Woodend office if you can see the old library. In addition to books for adults, it contains hundreds of stuffed American birds. The mansion is rented for weddings, bar mitzvahs, and other celebrations but is generally open on weekdays 9–5.

During family programs (which include parents), classes, and one- to two-week camps, educated naturalists foster environmental awareness and unlock nature's mysteries. Each program focuses on a nature-oriented theme, such as flying squirrels, meadow habitats, pond life, or "metamorphosis magic," and features hands-on activities like catching insects, fishing for pond creatures with nets, or investigating rotting log communities.

If you like this sight, you may also like Rock Creek Park (#19).

MAKE THE MOST OF YOUR TIME Wear old

clothes and apply sunscreen and bug repellent before you arrive. If you're with a little one and want to be able to use your stroller, head down the driveway from the parking lot. When you reach the huge walnut tree, you're near what some kids call the "secret pond." Every stick, leaf, rock, and insect needs to stay at Woodend. If your little collectors are disappointed by this rule, you can visit the bookshop. It sells souvenirs for young naturalists, including nature books, puzzles, T-shirts, and games.

BUREAU OF ENGRAVING AND PRINTING

 how me the money! It's here—some $907 million printed daily—and we defy you not to enjoy watching bills roll off the presses. Despite the lack of free samples, the guided, 35-minute bureau tour is one of the city's most popular attractions.

The United States began printing paper currency in 1862. Two men and four women separated and sealed by hand $1 and $2 U.S. notes printed by private companies. Today, the bureau employs approximately 2,500 people, who work out of this building and another in Fort Worth, Texas.

On tour, you can look through wide windows to see how money gets made. First, color is added to the paper. Then, both sides of the bills are printed in large 32- or 50-note sheets. Older machines print the back side first. Newer ones print front and back simultaneously. Next, machines inspect the notes for defects. (Bureau employees refer to bills as "notes.") For example, if a sheet was folded instead of flat during the process, notes may only be half

MAKE THE MOST OF YOUR TIME
March through August, required same-day timed-entry tickets are issued starting at 8 AM at the Raoul Wallenberg Place SW ticket booth. Waits to get in can be up to two hours, and if a tour bus arrives as you do, you may be stuck outside longer. September through February is off-peak time, so tickets aren't required and lineups likely aren't as long. While waiting, amuse your kids with some fun facts. For example: If you spent $1 every second, it would take 317 years to spend $10 billion; a mile-high stack of currency would contain over 14½ million notes.

THE CASTLE (SMITHSONIAN INSTITUTION BUILDING)

65

In London, castles may be for kings and queens. Here in Washington, the Castle is for us common folk who want to map out a day on the National Mall, a historic expanse of lawn between the Washington Monument and the Capitol Reflecting Pool. Popularly called the Castle because of its magnificent towers and turrets, this first Smithsonian building is a Norman-style structure made of red sandstone. Completed in 1855, it originally housed all of the Smithsonian's operations—hard to imagine now—including the science and art collections and the research laboratories. It was even home to the first Smithsonian secretary and his family.

In the 1880s, American buffalo (aka bison) were kept in a pen behind it. These once-numerous beasts had been hunted so relentlessly that numbers were dwindling. Determined to prevent their extinction, Samuel Pierpont Langley, the Smithsonian's third secretary, convinced Congress to provide a place where bison and other animals could be protected and displayed. This marked the beginning of the National Zoo.

MAKE THE MOST OF YOUR TIME

Since the Castle opens an hour and a half before the other Mall museums, early risers can get a good jump on their adventures. Early birds can also flock to the monuments on the Mall.

EATS FOR KIDS The following Smithsonian museums on the Mall have **food courts** (see each listing): the National Air and Space Museum, National Museum of American History, National Museum of the American Indian, and the National Museum of Natural History. But maybe what you really need to get going is a morning pastry and coffee or an afternoon ice cream in the Smithsonian's Castle.

14th and C Sts. SW.
Metro: Smithsonian (Independence Ave. exit)

 Free

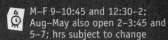
M–F 9–10:45 and 12:30–2;
Aug–May also open 2–3:45 and
5–7; hrs subject to change

202/874-2330 or 866/874-2330;
www.moneyfactory.gov

 5 and up

printed. Rejects are shredded and sold or recycled. In the final area, serial numbers and Federal Reserve seals are printed, and notes are cut.

Each $1 note costs 4¢–5.2¢ to print. Each $100 note costs about 13¢ because of security enhancements like watermarks, color-shifting ink, and security threads. Hold one of these bills up to the light to see the vertically embedded threads. Environmentally minded kids will be glad to learn no trees are cut to make paper currency; it's composed of 75% cotton and 25% linen.

It may sound crazy to adults, but kids like to buy shredded money in the gift shop. A small bag costing a few bucks contains $150 worth of bills that didn't pass inspection. For about $5 your children can get slightly more practical mementos: postcards that look like currency with their photos on them.

If you like this sight, you may also like the National Gallery of Art (#36), where you can see paintings of some of the men on the money.

KEEP IN MIND
Would you like to make money? Ten-year-old Emma Brown did. She was the youngest employee in bureau history, but she didn't work here for the fun of it. Emma's brother, the family breadwinner, was killed in action during the Civil War, leaving the girl to care for her disabled mother and the rest of the family. Emma's congressman gave her a political appointment so she could make money by making money.

EATS FOR KIDS
The **U.S. Department of Agriculture Cafeteria** (12th and C Sts. SW, tel. 202/488-7279) has something for everyone. Show your ID and get visitor stickers at the front desk, then choose from seven food stations and a buffet. Choices include grilled cheese and hot meals with veggies.

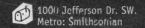 1000 Jefferson Dr. SW.
Metro: Smithsonian

 Free

 Daily 8:30–5:30

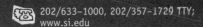 202/633–1000, 202/357–1729 TTY;
www.si.edu

 2 and up

Start at the Castle's Smithsonian Information Center, where you can learn all about the sprawling museum, education, and research facility. Comprising 19 museums and galleries (10 of them on the National Mall) plus a zoo, the Washington area's Smithsonian Institution is the largest museum complex in the world. A 10 minute video overview plays constantly (if your kids will sit still that long, you may get to watch it). Better yet, talk to the knowledgeable volunteers or pick up a brochure. Touch-screen monitors at heights for both children and adults display visitor service information. Interactive videos provide more details about the museums plus other D.C. attractions. Push a button on the electronic map to locate Arlington National Cemetery or light up the entire Metro system. There's also a scale model of the National Mall and a Braille city map, which wasn't designed for children, but draws them nonetheless.

If you like this sight for its castle-like construction, you may also like the exhibits at the National Building Museum (#38). They focus on architecture, engineering, and design.

KEEP IN MIND You can't see the Smithsonian's entire collection of objects, artifacts, specimens, and creatures—137 million and growing, due to gifts, purchases, and, at the zoo, births—because only an estimated 1%–2% of the collections is on display at any time. Luckily, unlike the stuff under kids' beds, the remaining objects are carefully cataloged and used in research. If you're short on time, stop by the Commons to view America's Treasure Chest, which provides a sampling of objects from each museum.

64

Back in the 1770s, children didn't have to go to school, wear shoes, or take a nightly bath. Some contemporary kids might think those early days were easy—that is, until they visit this re-created Colonial farm. When school is closed, young volunteers portraying Colonial children explain how working all day on the farm kept them from attending classes. Those who could fit into one of the few pairs of shoes a family might own were lucky, as they were less likely to suffer from sore feet. Frequent baths weren't considered healthful—nor were they practical, since heating enough water for a tub took a long time.

Even when the Colonial kids aren't here, you and your children can watch a pair of historical interpreters, dressed in period clothing, demonstrate how a farming couple eked out a living by tending to tobacco and wheat fields, a vegetable garden, farm animals, and family chores.

A dirt path winds around an orchard, fields, a tobacco barn, a pond, a hog pen, and an English-style one-room farmhouse. The walk is comfortable, and a well-napped preschooler

MAKE THE MOST OF YOUR TIME Encourage your little ones to go to the bathroom before you arrive. The farm is equipped with the modern-day equivalent of outhouses (in other words, portable toilets).

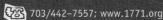
can make the trip. Pushing a stroller along the root-laced path is tricky, but it is possible.

During Market Fairs, held the third full weekends in May, July, and October, families enjoy making Colonial crafts (about $1 each), watching puppet shows, and other timeless pastimes. And just as in the 1770s, you can eat and shop. Check out the rosemary chicken and vegetables roasted over a fire, fresh-baked pies, and more. Reproductions of 18th-century pottery, jewelry, fragrant soaps, clothing, and toys are for sale on Market Fair days.

If you like this sight, you may also like the National Colonial Farm in Accokeek, Maryland, on the shore of the Potomac River directly across from Mount Vernon (tel. 301/283–2113; www.accokeek.org).

KEEP IN MIND

When Colonial kids played, they either used their imaginations or made toys out of things that had no monetary value and weren't needed elsewhere. They crafted marbles out of clay and turned split sapling trees into hoops, which they then rolled on the ground with a stick. Try rolling a Hula-Hoop with a stick yourself. It's harder than you might think.

EATS FOR KIDS If you packed a lunch, grab one of the picnic tables at the farm entrance. A few miles away, the **McLean Family Restaurant** (1321 Chain Bridge Rd., tel. 703/356–9883) has been serving Greek and American dishes for more than 35 years. At **Rocco's Italian Restaurant** (1357 Chain Bridge Rd., tel. 703/821–3736), child-size pizzas are best sellers, but those with more sophisticated palates can order manicotti, rigatoni, and ravioli. After eating, kids (and adults) can get a lollipop for the road.

COLLEGE PARK AVIATION MUSEUM

Walk by the animatronic Wilbur Wright and he'll tell you about the thrills and chills of teaching pilots to fly in 1909. Of course, children don't have to take Wilbur's word for it: They'll see it for themselves at this interactive museum dedicated to early aviation.

Your kids will be challenged and exhilarated as they turn and pull levers, knobs, and switches on flight simulators. They can try starting a plane's engine, not by turning a key as is done today, but the way it was done before World War I, by turning a propeller. (Hint: Make sure no one is in the way and push down as hard as you can. Then step back. It's loud!) Kids can even dress like pilots of yore, donning goggles, silk scarves, helmets, and flight jackets to pose for pictures against an airplane backdrop.

A full-scale replica of the 1911 Wright B Aeroplane, a restored 1918 Curtiss Jenny, a 1932-era Monocoupe, and a Berliner Helicopter grace the largest gallery of this airy museum, which opened in 1998. If you notice a similarity to the National Air and Space Museum, you're not imagining it—both were designed by the same architectural firm. But here

KEEP IN MIND

This museum is the place our readers say they're happiest to hear about. The nearest Metro stop is about a 10-minute walk through an industrial area and, being on the Green Line, it means a transfer for many people. Fortunately, parking is plentiful and free.

MAKE THE MOST OF YOUR TIME

For a list of what's happening on the day you visit, check the flight desk at the front of the museum. It may list How Things Fly (of interest to older kids) or Peter Pan Club (activities for preschoolers, like making paper airplanes). In addition, when Maryland or Prince George's County public schools are closed, the museum sponsors aviation craft activities. If you don't make your own souvenir, you may want to take home a flight of fancy from the museum's gift shop, which is full of themed toys and games, many under $5.

1985 Cpl. Frank Scott Dr., College Park, MD.
Metro: College Park

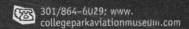
301/864–6029; www.
collegeparkaviationmuseum.com

\$4, \$2
children
2–18 and
students

Daily 10–5

2 and up

you can see and do everything in an hour, and you won't have to worry about losing your children in crowds.

Before leaving the building, amateur aviators can "pitch" and "roll" the hand controls of the Wright Experience Flight Simulator to maneuver turns and gain altitude while flying over computerized 3-D images of this airport as it appeared when the Wright Brothers first taught military pilots to fly. Instant replay lets the pilots experience their crash or successful landing again.

Outside there's more in store. Children five and under can get a feel for flying by riding around in wooden planes on a mini-runway. Gaze out the museum's large glass wall onto College Park Airport, the world's oldest continually operating airport.

If you like this sight, you may also like the National Air and Space Museum (#42).

EATS FOR KIDS If your kids like to watch planes, bring lunch and eat on the museum balcony, overlooking the airport. You'll need to get back in the car for restaurant fare, but this college town offers a lot of cheap choices. Chocolate-chip pancakes and other breakfast foods are served all day at **Plato's Diner** (7150 Baltimore Ave., tel. 301/779–7070). A plate of noodles will set you back less than \$5 at **Noodles and Company** (7320 Baltimore Ave. Rte. 1, tel. 301/779–5300).

CORCORAN GALLERY OF ART

Create a flip-book like the flip art in this book. Style your own fashion photo shoot. Turn everyday objects into works of art. These are some of the activities offered when you participate in family programs at one of the oldest U.S. museums.

During the Corcoran's annual Family Day, the museum becomes an intergenerational funfest with music, dancing, crafts, and face painting. Classes and camps for children as young as five are also available throughout the year. They're led by credentialed art teachers who turn their young charges into watercolorists, collage artists, and fashion designers inspired by the Corcoran's collection.

If you can't make one of these events, you can still create a fun family adventure by sharing your enthusiasm for art with your children. The permanent collection at the Corcoran (one of the few large, private museums in Washington outside the Smithsonian family) numbers more than 14,000 works, including paintings by the first great American portraitists: John Singleton Copley, Gilbert Stuart, and Rembrandt Peale.

MAKE THE MOST OF YOUR TIME If you're up for another art gallery, the much smaller but free Renwick Gallery (8th and F Sts., tel. 202/633-7970; www.americanart.si.edu) is only a few blocks away. Lots of kids like *Game Fish* by Larry Fuente, because the mixed media piece is made of hundreds of little gaming pieces, such as dice, blocks, and darts.

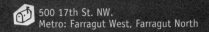
500 17th St. NW.
Metro: Farragut West, Farragut North

202/639–1700; www.corcoran.org

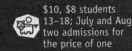
$10, $8 students
13–18; July and Aug
two admissions for
the price of one

W–Su 10–5

5 and up

In fact, the portrait on the $1 bill was modeled on Stuart's *Portrait of George Washington*. A replica (by the artist's own hand) is at the gallery. There's also a huge painting, *George Washington Before Yorktown,* by Rembrandt Peale. One of 17 children, five of whom were named for artists, Peale took some liberties with reality. Washington's horse, Nelson, was actually brown, but Peale painted him white, perhaps to stand out against the mainly brown background. (Incidentally, at times Washington did own white horses.) Ask at the front desk if these paintings of Washington are hanging that day; if they are, hand your kids dollar bills and have them try to find them.

The Corcoran staff recommends these "games" for kids: Imagine!, which involves pretending you can jump inside the painting and describe what you might see, hear, and smell; and Re-title it!, where you look at a title the artist used and then make up your own.

If you like this sight, you may also like the National Museum of Women in the Arts (#27).

KEEP IN MIND

Ask at the front desk for a copy of the family guide. If the Salon Doré isn't included in the guide, take a peek at this gorgeous gilded room where walls display something surprising—sports equipment and musical instruments.

EATS FOR KIDS Specializing in food from local sources, **Todd Gray's Muse at the Corcoran** (tel. 202/639–1786) offers high chairs and counter service. The restaurant's Market Brunch, with live music on Sunday, is a festive event for families. If you'd rather dine on paper plates than china, **Burrito Brothers** (1825 I St. NW, tel. 202/887–8266), a Mexican fast-food restaurant, is a few blocks away in the Ronald Reagan Building. For other casual eateries, *see* the DAR Museum and the White House.

DAR MUSEUM

Back in Colonial days, many boys wore dresses until they were about seven-years old and many kids were expected to empty chamber pots in the morning as part of their chores. Oh, they didn't get Christmas presents either: Gift exchanging was originally something reserved for adults.

Guides and docents at the DAR (Daughters of the American Revolution) Museum dispel any myths that life was all frilly and fancy 200 years ago or B.C. (before computers)—even though there's plenty of finery to see here.

Modern families can sample early American life during Fun Family Saturdays and leave with a craft as a souvenir. Colonial Adventure, for children five to eight, is another engaging program.

Participants get started by dressing the part. Boys wear vests and three-corner caps. (Don't worry. Skirts aren't even available for boys.) Girls don long white aprons, because

MAKE THE MOST OF YOUR TIME

If your children have particular interests, inform a docent. Those with an ear for music should definitely see the antique instruments in the Rhode Island room. In wealthy homes, parents often encouraged daughters to play a keyboard instrument and sons to play the flute or violin.

EATS FOR KIDS The wait may be a little long at noon but so is the list of selections at the nearby **Bread Line** (1751 Pennsylvania Ave. NW, tel. 202/822–8900), where you can get smoothies, sandwiches, fresh-baked breads, bagels, and muffins (all made on-site) any weekday. Grabbing a quick bite at the **Clara Barton Café** is another tasty possibility. Open 7–2 Monday through Friday, it is located in the American Red Cross building (1730 E St. NW) and named for that organization's founder.

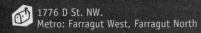 1776 D St. NW.
Metro: Farragut West, Farragut North

 202/879-3241;
www.dar.org/museum

 Free

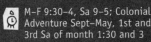 M–F 9:30–4, Sa 9–5; Colonial
Adventure Sept–May, 1st and
3rd Sa of month 1:30 and 3

 5 and up

proper Colonial ladies never showed their ankles. Docents, who are all DAR members and who also wear Colonial garb, then lead the children on a special tour, describing life in Colonial days.

While the younger ones are off exploring, parents and older siblings can take their own guided tour through 18th-century America (tours run M–F 9:30–4, Sa 9–5). Appropriately, docents weave tales of women's contributions into their descriptions as they showcase various museum rooms.

Your kids might be impressed by the Oklahoma room, replicating a Colonial kitchen, or the Georgia room, set up like a Savannah tavern where citizens gathered for the state's first reading of the Declaration of Independence. In the New Hampshire room, docents describe 18th- and 19th-century dolls. And the Wisconsin room depicts a one-room house like those that only fortunate families could afford in Colonial times.

If you like this sight, you may also like the Children's Museum of Rose Hill Manor Park (1611 North Market St., Frederick, MD, tel. 301/600–1650; www.rosehillmuseum.com).

KEEP IN MIND Parents often enjoy Colonial Adventure and family day activities as much as their children. If you can't time your visit to coincide with a scheduled program, be sure to pick up the Family Self-Guide brochure and don't miss the Touch of Independence room where everything is—you guessed it—touchable.

D.C. DUCKS

What do you get when you cross a tour bus with a boat? A duck, of course—a D.C. Duck, that is. Your family can see the city by both land and water without leaving your seats aboard these unusual amphibious vehicles: Standard 2½-ton GM trucks in watertight shells with propellers and room for 28 intrepid passengers.

During the 1½-hour ride, a wise-quacking captain entertains with anecdotes and historical trivia about Washington's memorials, monuments, and historic buildings. You may even be quizzed about sights along the way. Answer correctly and ding—the bell rings! For example, the captain may ask what boats are represented by the three flags near the statue of Christopher Columbus in front of Union Station. No, the answer isn't the *Love Boat,* the S.S. *Minnow,* and the *Titanic,* but rather the *Niña,* the *Pinta,* and *the Santa María.*

Ducks, known as DUKWs in World War II, were created to transport soldiers and supplies from ships to areas without ports. During the war more than 21,000 were produced, mostly

MAKE THE MOST OF YOUR TIME If your family is more into bikes than boats or if you'd just like to see the city a different way, consider a Bike and Roll tour (1100 Pennsylvania Ave. or 50 Massachusetts Ave., tel. 202/842–2453; www.bikeandroll. com). For $40 per adult, $30 for kids 12 and under (including use of a bike), you can take a three-hour tour covering approximately 8 miles and 55 sights. Along the way, a guide discusses history, lore, and even scandals of the capital city. The trip is appropriate for ages seven and older, and reservations are recommended.

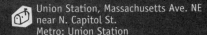
Union Station, Massachusetts Ave. NE
near N. Capitol St.
Metro: Union Station

202/832-9800 or 855/323-8257;
www.dcducks.com

$39, $29 under 12

Apr–Oct, daily 10–5 (occasionally
later); M–F departures hourly,
Sa–Su every ½ hr

4 and up

by women. After it ended, the Army left many DUKWs abroad, and they can still be found around the world.

Starting along the city streets, the Duck keeps pace with traffic. Eventually it moves into the Potomac River, allowing your children to glimpse the Pentagon, the Anacostia Helicopter Station (home of the presidential helicopters), and the War College, formerly Fort McNair, where the conspirators who plotted to kill Lincoln were tried, convicted, and hanged. Often children are invited to take the captain's seat and steer the Duck. The part of the tour that really quacks kids up, though, is quacking themselves—both at tourists in town and real ducks on the water.

If you like this ride, you may also like riding the ostrich on the historic carousel at Glen Echo Park (#55).

KEEP IN MIND The United States Coast Guard requires that the DUCKS devote one seat per passenger regardless of age, so everyone on board must have a ticket. They go on sale at 9 AM, an hour before the first tour begins.

EATS FOR KIDS When tummies rumble, duck into Union Station (tel. 202/289–1908; www.unionstationdc.com). At this bustling train station, where inaugural balls have been held, you'll find more than 35 vendors offering fast food from around the world. Top family picks include **Chipotle** (tel. 202/706–5935) and **Johnny Rockets** (tel. 202/289–6969). Washington-inspired chocolates from the **America!** store (tel. 202/842–0540) provide a sweet finish. You can purchase one bar for $3 or a package of 10 small ones to share for about $9.

DISCOVERY THEATER

59

In the midst of the Mall's mammoth museums you'll find a small theater, just west of the Castle (*see* #65), that brings both our national heritage and other cultures to life. At the S. Dillon Ripley Center kids can delight in entertaining and educational performances, including festive dances from around the globe, rock concerts for toddlers, and beautiful, boisterous puppet shows. On a more serious note, history opens up as kids watch plays like *How Old is a Hero*, about Ruby Bridges and other children of the Civil Rights movement. From popular tales to well-told, lesser-known ones, the Smithsonian's Discovery Theater lives up to its name.

Young audiences are often encouraged to take part by singing, clapping, or helping to develop characters and plots. And because you're never more than a dozen rows away from the action (the theater seats 200 people max), close encounters between the audience and actors are easy.

Though most performances are geared to preschoolers through sixth-graders, some are for older children and teens. Many of these are held in the 550-seat Baird Auditorium

KEEP IN MIND
Ride a painted pony on a carousel in front of the building. The lone dragon is the most desired mount and sometimes kids will let others go ahead of them so they're first in line for it on the next cycle.

MAKE THE MOST OF YOUR TIME
You can connect with the theater through Facebook (Smithsonian's Discovery Theater) or Twitter (@SmithsonianKids). Otherwise, go to their website for info or check the "Weekend" section of the *Washington Post*, which lists kid-oriented productions around town. No matter what show you select, reservations are recommended as they often sell out and walk-up tickets are not guaranteed. Plan to arrive 15 minutes early. If you're attending a 10 AM show, go around to the west entrance in the Enid A. Haupt Garden. Doors there open early for Discovery Theater patrons only: The building itself doesn't open until 10.

S. Dillon Ripley Center, 1100 Jefferson Dr. SW.
Metro: Smithsonian

 $6, $5 ages 3–17

202/633–8700; www.
discoverytheater.org

Late Sept–late July, M–F
10 and 11:30, Sa 12

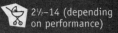 2½–14 (depending
on performance)

at the National Museum of Natural History (*see* #29). Performances for older kids tend to be tied to local schools' curricula and revolve around historical figures or events. Past examples have included *African Roots*, *Latino Soul* (about making your way as multiracial in an American high school) and *Sacagawea's Sisters* (about a pioneering Shoshone woman).

Throughout the year, Discovery Theater also celebrates cultural heritage. In February, for example, African American History Month is marked with songs, stories, and performances on the Mall, and with a tour of an original Discovery Theater play like *Black Diamond: Satchel Paige and the Negro Leagues*. December brings the most popular show *Seasons of Light*, introducing traditional celebrations such as Devali, Ramadan, Sankta Lucia, Chanukah, Las Posadas, Kwanzaa and Native American Solstice rituals. The interactive production has sold out more than 30 shows a year for 14 years!

If you like this sight, you may also like the plays and puppet shows at Glen Echo Park (#55).

EATS FOR KIDS For a hot pretzel or an ice cream, check out the **street vendors** in front of the building. For a complete meal, walk past the Castle and down a block to the National Air and Space Museum's restaurants, about five minutes away (*see* #42). Across the Mall, both the National Museum of Natural History and the National Museum of American History also have restaurants (*see* #29 and #32).

FORD'S THEATRE
NATIONAL HISTORIC SITE

The events of April 14, 1865, which shocked the nation and closed this theater, continue to fascinate both young and old. On that night, during a performance of *Our American Cousin,* John Wilkes Booth entered the state box on the balcony and assassinated Abraham Lincoln. The stricken president was carried across the street to the house of tailor William Peterson, where he died the next morning.

After reopening following renovations in 2009, tickets are required—but free—to tour this site. (Note that the ticket office opens at 8:30 AM. Guided tours depart on the hour and half hour.) Allow about an hour to go through the Lincoln Museum in the lower level and hear a National Park Service ranger's interpretation of the night Lincoln was shot.

In the museum, there are plenty of artifacts about the traumatic event, but the Derringer pistol that Booth used and the life-size statues of people looking to Lincoln for jobs seem to attract the most attentions. To get kids ages 6 to 12 interested in exploring further,

MAKE THE MOST OF YOUR TIME Every year from Thanksgiving through New Year's, the ghosts of Christmases past, present, and future come to the Ford's Theatre stage in Charles Dickens's classic tale *A Christmas Carol.* (The rest of the year, performances tend to be serious adult plays.) Call 202/347–4833 for information.

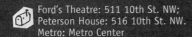

pick up a Junior Ranger handout. Those who complete the activities can pick up a prize at the end.

Your ticket also entitles you to cross the street to the Peterson House (where Lincoln finally succumbed) and the Center for Education and Leadership. The Center, which opened in 2012, picks up the story of what happened after Lincoln died and ends with a look at his legacy. Its centerpiece is an eye-popping, three-story tower of made up of 6,800 books written about the slain president.

If you like this sight, you may also be interested in seeing the actual bullet that killed Lincoln, on display at the National Museum of Health and Medicine (#30), or touring the home of Lincoln's friend, abolitionist Frederick Douglass (#56).

KEEP IN MIND
If your child is tired or cranky, note that visiting the Peterson House and the Center for Education and Leadership will probably add at least another 25 minutes to your tour.

EATS FOR KIDS Older kids will love the **Hard Rock Cafe** (999 E St. NW, tel. 202/737-7625), which mixes meals with music and rock memorabilia. For soups, salads, and signature toasted sandwiches, check out **Potbelly** (555 12th St., tel. 202/347-7100). The restaurant's "Wreck" sandwich is loaded with a variety of meats. Its "Big Jack," may sound intimidating but is actually a classic PB&J. If you order water with your meal, you'll be enjoying one of Honest Abe's favorite beverages.

FRANKLIN DELANO ROOSEVELT MEMORIAL

If you visit this memorial to our 32nd president with older children, take your time walking through its four outdoor "rooms" or galleries—each symbolic of one of Roosevelt's four terms. Waterfalls and reflecting pools are interspersed throughout and are great for dangling toes. Pause in the granite passageways between the galleries. They're engraved with some of Roosevelt's most famous quotes, including "The only thing we have to fear is fear itself." If you come with toddlers, however, head straight to the third room where they can pet a statue of Roosevelt's beloved dog Fala.

Afterward, challenge your children to look closely at the big bronze wall of faces in the second room: It depicts people put back to work after the Depression. See if you can find two men planting trees, an artist stirring paint, one farmer gathering oranges, and another driving a tractor. There's even a girl painting and a boy sculpting. Also in the second gallery, handprints along the columns, representing the working hands of the American people,

MAKE THE MOST OF YOUR TIME

This memorial is one of the best places for a family photo op. Take your place in the Breadline, listen to Roosevelt's fireside chat, or pet Fala (you'll notice that the tips of the adorable Scottish terrier's ears already shine from all the attention).

EATS FOR KIDS You might find one of Roosevelt's favorite foods (hot dogs) at a **food stand** near the Lincoln Memorial. You might find another (fish chowder) a short drive away at **Maine Avenue Seafood Market** (1100 Maine Ave. SW, tel. 202/484–2722), which carries fresh fish and shellfish. Maine Avenue also contains seven waterside restaurants, including local seafood powerhouse **Phillips Flagship** (900 Water St. SW, tel. 202/488–8515). All have terraces overlooking the Washington Channel and the boats moored there.

1850 W. Basin Dr. SW,
west side of Tidal Basin.
Metro: Smithsonian

 Free

 24 hrs; staffed daily 9:30 AM–11:30 PM

202/426-6841; www.nps.gov/fdrm

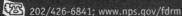 2 and up

encourage you to touch. In the fourth room, a statue honors first lady Eleanor Roosevelt, a shy child who grew into a vocal spokesperson for human rights.

More than recognizing FDR's contributions, the memorial teaches children about history, war, and even disability. Due to polio, Roosevelt used a wheelchair for the last 24 years of his life, and a statue of him in a wheelchair was added to the memorial in 2001 after years of controversy. Ask an older child what's more important: that Roosevelt be portrayed realistically and as a role model for the disabled or that his desire not to have people see his disability be honored?

If you like this sight, you may also want to see the original monument to Roosevelt in front of the National Archives Building (#39): It was made to order. Roosevelt said if anyone put up a memorial to him, he would want it to be about the size of a desk.

KEEP IN MIND If Roosevelt's dog makes more of an impression on your little one than the president himself does, don't be surprised. Many kids in the 1940s reacted the same way. Fala was a famous pooch in his day. He sat at the feet of his master and British Prime Minister Winston Churchill when they signed the Atlantic Charter in 1941. For merchandise featuring the presidential pooch, check out the bookstore. A portion of the proceeds benefits the National Park Service.

FREDERICK DOUGLASS
NATIONAL HISTORIC SITE

56

Okay. Time to pay tribute to another influential American, Frederick Douglass. Pick up tickets for a 30-minute tour in the visitor center, where a wall is devoted to this prolific speaker and writer's quotations. Among his more famous utterances is, "I would unite with anybody to do right and with nobody to do wrong." Here your children can shake hands with the bronze statue of Douglass, see the Douglass family tree, and browse through a gift shop filled with Douglass-related books.

Next you can learn his backstory by watching the 17-minute film *Fighter for Freedom: The Frederick Douglass Story*. Douglass knew neither his mother, a slave, nor the identity of his father, a white man. At age eight, he was sent to work for a family in Baltimore, where he was exposed to the "mystery of reading" and decided that education was "the pathway to freedom." At 20 he escaped and became an abolitionist, women's rights activist, author, editor of an antislavery newspaper, minister to Haiti, and the most respected 19th-century African American orator.

KEEP IN MIND You'll need a ticket to get inside Douglass' home. They're free but reservations are required for groups of 10 or more (tel. 877/559–6777) and strongly recommended for everyone else (tel. 877/444-6777; www.recreation.gov). A $1.50 charge applies per reservation.

1411 W St. SE.
Metro: Anacostia, then B2 bus

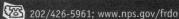
Free

Apr–Oct, daily 9–5; tours at 9, 12:15, 1:15, 3, 3:30, and 4 (Nov–Mar, closes at 4; last tour at 3:30)

202/426-5961; www.nps.gov/frdo

9 and up

After the film, follow a park ranger to Cedar Hill, the first designated African American National Historic Site and Douglass' final home.

Rangers focus on his life at Cedar Hill, first with Anna Murray, his wife of 40 years, and, after her death, with second wife, Helen Pitts, a white woman who was 20 years his junior. Douglass simply explained that his first wife was the color of his mother, his second the color of his father. Though the tour is best for children who have studied American history, rangers are skilled at engaging even kindergartners. Children learn not only about the past but also about the importance of freedom and equality today.

If you like this sight, you may also like another old home at Sully Historic Site (#14).

EATS FOR KIDS
Unfortunately, the only place you are allowed to eat here is on the grassy hill near the visitor center, next to the parking lot, but there are no picnic tables. So you might want to munch on something before or after your visit.

MAKE THE MOST OF YOUR TIME
Though *Fighter for Freedom: The Frederick Douglass Story* is enlightening, this short film depicts a graphic beating Douglass got when he was a slave. Some children and even adults find it disturbing, not just because of the violence but because it confronts a shameful part of our history. Encourage your kids to talk about their feelings and ask questions of you and the rangers. To enhance your children's appreciation of Cedar Hill, talk about Frederick Douglass, the Civil War, and the Civil Rights movement before you arrive.

GLEN ECHO PARK

The 1921 Dentzel Carousel alone would be reason enough to visit this historic spot. Located in the center of the park, the vintage ride offers a choice of mounts, which range from a painted pony and a majestic lion to a saber-toothed tiger and an ostrich. Like the carousel, the park offers lots of options for families.

For starters, the arts thrive here. The Adventure Theatre MTC stages children's productions like *A Little House Christmas, Cat in the Hat,* and *Winnie the Pooh* year-round in a 165-seat theater. At the Puppet Co. Playhouse (a 250-seat venue made specifically for puppet shows), nationally acclaimed puppeteers manipulate a variety of puppets in classic plays and stories. At least twice a week, the Playhouse hosts Tiny Tots @ 10 for wee ones up to four years old ($5 for all ages). If you're coming in winter, try to catch *Nutcracker,* one of the theater's most popular productions. Reservations are recommended.

EATS FOR KIDS

When the carousel at Glen Echo is open (May–Sept, W–Th 10–2 and Sa–Su 12–6; Sept–Oct, Sa–Su 12–6), so is the adjacent **snack bar.** But whether you bring or buy food, you'll find enough **picnic tables** and wide-open spaces here to accommodate scores of families.

MAKE THE MOST OF YOUR TIME
Whatever event you're going to at Glen Echo, allow at least an extra 30 minutes. Just stomping over the bridge leading to the park takes time. You also may want to act out the Norwegian folktale of Billy Goats Gruff, toss stones in the creek, and take a spin around the carousel.

7300 MacArthur Blvd., at Goldsboro Rd.,
Glen Echo, MD

 301/634-2222, 301/634-5380
(Puppet Co.); www.glenechopark.org

Clara Barton
National Historic
Site free; carousel
$1.25; plays $19

 Daily 9–5; puppet shows Th–F 10 and
11:30, Sa–Su 11:30 and 1; plays Sa–Su
11 and 2 (weekdays vary)

All ages

Nature holds its own at Glen Echo Park: A local Eagle Scout candidate established nature trails around Minnehaha Creek, near the museum. History has its place, too, and children who have studied the Civil War or women's history may enjoy a tour of the Clara Barton National Historic Site, near the park entrance. Known as the "Angel of the Battlefield" for nursing wounded soldiers, Barton founded the American Red Cross. Rangers conduct hourly tours that give insight into her life and Glen Echo at the turn of the last century.

Finally, the park is also a great spot for recreation. When your kids need to let off steam, there's plenty of space to run around and a playground with swings, slides, and a climbing tower.

If you like this sight, you might also like the plays at Discovery Theater (#59).

KEEP IN MIND There are more than kids' activities at this park, founded by two brothers who invented the eggbeater. It's the adults who kick up their heels in the historic Spanish Ballroom. All dance events are open to the public, and most include a mini-lesson. Whether waltz, contra, salsa, or swing is your thing, you can find it here.

GODDARD SPACE FLIGHT
VISITOR CENTER

Not nearly as large or crowded as the Smithsonian's National Air and Space Museums, this NASA-run venue brings space flight down to earth while letting imaginations soar.

Sign in at the front desk where friendly staff members are eager to answer questions about the Center. Having been renovated in 2012, it now has more gee-whiz gadgetry plus interactive displays on subjects like planets, black holes, and the Hubble space telescope that will appeal to everyone from preschoolers to professional scientists.

A replica of a *Gemini* spacecraft, similar to the one astronauts Buzz Aldrin and Jim Lovell spent four days in, is as good as real for youngsters who can "take flight" inside the compact car-size capsule. Those who want to look authentic can even request orange spacesuits at the front desk.

MAKE THE MOST OF YOUR TIME Bring your own rocket to model rocket launches on the first Sunday of the month at 1. Goddard's gift shop sells some, but you'd need about a half hour to assemble the rocket and another 24 hours to let the glue dry. The site also hosts Experiment Days for elementary-school-age children one Sunday each month (usually the third), September through June from 1 to 3.

  8800 Greenbelt Rd., Greenbelt, MD

301/286–9041; www.nasa.gov/ centers/goddard/visitor/home

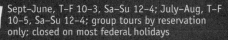 Free

Sept–June, T–F 10–3, Sa–Su 12–4; July–Aug, T–F 10–5, Sa–Su 12–4; group tours by reservation only; closed on most federal holidays

 2 and up

Kids may also touch a plasma ball (older ones who read can find out how common this matter is in space), then feel for themselves the impact of insulation in space, and find out how old the universe really is (think billions of years).

Before exiting, be sure to check out Science on a Sphere. Using computers and video projectors, you can see animated movies and images of the Earth, other planets, the sun, and the stars on a 6-foot sphere that looks like it is floating. Short movies repeat every two hours.

Outside the center is a "rocket garden," with a real 92-foot Delta rocket and other authentic space hardware. You can also see other buildings at this sprawling government complex where scientists and engineers monitor spaceships circling the Earth, the solar system, and beyond.

If you like this sight, you may also like the College Park Aviation Museum (#63), which is about 10 minutes away.

KEEP IN MIND
Goddard is about 9 miles from Washington, but off the beaten path. From the Baltimore–Washington Parkway (I–295) or Capital Beltway, exit to Route 193 east (Greenbelt Road). Turn north off Greenbelt Road onto ICESat Road, then left on WMAP Road into the large, free parking lot.

EATS FOR KIDS Unlike so many museums, you don't have to walk through the gift shop to leave this one. Beyond a few candies, though, the only edible items sold in it are astronaut-style freeze-dried ice-cream sandwiches (messy things that aren't particularly tasty but cool to kids). If you bring your own food, you'll find **picnic tables** in the shade and the sun. A short drive away in historic Greenbelt, the **New Deal Café** (113 Center Way, tel. 301/474–5642) gives parents a break. While waiting for your soups, sandwiches, or vegetarian—even vegan—entrées, your kids can read books, play board games, or work on puzzles.

GREAT FALLS

T hanks to the Ice Age 2-million years ago, a wide, flat, slow-moving body of water cut its way through bedrock and created Great Falls, a lovely cascade on the Potomac adjacent to the C&O Canal National Historical Park (tel. 202/653–5190; www.nps.gov/choh). Here the water thrashes about faster, frothier, and noisier than the wildest bubble bath, although your kids might want to test that theory come tub time!

For information and a trail map, head to the 1831 Tavern, which stopped providing food and shelter in the 1930s but still welcomes visitors. Exhibits cover how locks work, early canal life, plus indigenous plants and animals. The main attraction at this park, however, is the great outdoors.

If it's hiking you're after, check out these interesting options—just beware of trails too rugged for little ones. The Billy Goat Trail sounds simple, but the 4-mile loop requires scrambling over boulders. Hiking boots and athletic ability are recommended. The Gold

KEEP IN MIND

Ready for a mule-drawn boat ride? Although you go less than a mile, guides in 19th-century garb make it feel like time travel. Rides ($8 for ages 15 and up, $5 for ages 4–14) begin in April and usually run through summer. Call ahead to be sure.

MAKE THE MOST OF YOUR TIME
You can enjoy the falls from either Maryland or Virginia (9200 Old Dominion Dr., McLean, VA, tel. 703/285–2965). The Virginia side offers more opportunities for serious rock climbers. Bring your own equipment and register at the visitor center. Swimming and wading are prohibited on both sides, but you can fish (license required for anglers 16 and older), climb rocks, or go white-water kayaking. Kayaking is for experienced boaters and below the falls only, as currents are deadly. Despite signs and warnings, people occasionally dare the water, and lose.

Mine Loop also runs a little over 3 miles, revealing the remains of an 1867–1939 mine. (Not everyone went to California for gold!) Sorry, panning isn't allowed today.

For a golden view of the falls that everyone enjoys, take the walkway to Olmsted Island. This 0.6-mile, wheelchair- and stroller-accessible route leads to a platform with a spectacular view of the churning waters. Along the walkway, signs alert you to ancient plants growing among the rocks. You might also see more recent arrivals: freshwater Asiatic clamshells, first reported here in the 1980s. In any case, your kids can find a cozy seat on the rocks in the middle of the platform or on the benches from which you can see Mother Nature at her wildest.

If you like this sight, you may also like the United States National Arboretum (#8).

EATS FOR KIDS As at all National Park Service sites, you're not allowed to feed the animals, but you can feed yourselves. Buy something at the **snack bar** (open W–Su June–July and most weekends Mar–May and Sept–Nov), a few paces north of the tavern, or bring your own picnic. Potomac Village, 3½ miles away, has two supermarkets that sell prepared foods: **Giant** (9812 Falls Rd., tel. 301/983–4246) and **Safeway** (10104 River Rd., tel. 301/983–2150). Alternately, you can head to locally owned **Potomac Pizza** (9812 Falls Rd., tel. 301/299–7700), for pizza, calzones, and sub sandwiches.

HIRSHHORN MUSEUM
AND SCULPTURE GARDEN

Any child who thinks art museums only display boring, two-dimensional portraits of old-fashioned people is in for a surprise at the Hirshhorn. Art here isn't simply paint on canvas. Some is created from mud, twigs, leaves, stone, light, video monitors, and even fat. Here paper flowers grow out of a wall and a fish made of metal and glass seemingly swims on a brightly colored mobile.

American icons such as Georgia O'Keeffe, Jackson Pollock, Mark Rothko, Frank Stella, and Andy Warhol are represented along with modern European and Latin masters, including Juan Muñoz, René Magritte, and Joan Miró. Through acquisitions, the Hirshhorn continually adds work to its collection, and contemporary pieces by Robert Gober, Ann Hamilton, Jim Hodges, Ernesto Neto, Ed Ruscha, and numerous others reflect the diversity of technique and expression among today's artists.

Admittedly most kids won't recognize or particularly care about these names. So to make your museum experience fun, visit the information desk for a free Family Guide. It's full

MAKE THE MOST OF YOUR TIME Some of the coolest art for kids is outside in the Sculpture Garden. *Man Passing Through the Door* by Jean Ipousteguy may remind "muggles" of when Harry Potter boarded the train to Hogwarts, though instead of an owl, said man has another animal with him. Also ask your kids to find Kenneth Snelson's tall sculpture *Needle Tower* in the plaza. Get in its center, and look up. You'll see a star.

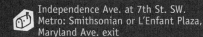
Independence Ave. at 7th St. SW.
Metro: Smithsonian or L'Enfant Plaza,
Maryland Ave. exit

 Free

202/633–1000, 202/357–1729 TTY;
www.hirshhorn.si.edu

Daily 10–5:30; Sculpture Garden
daily 7:30–sunset

5 and up; Young at Art
3–12; Artlab 13–18

of colorful art cards that encourage children to search for a work, learn something about it, and relate it to their own lives and imagination. For example, on the card about Claes Oldenburg's *Geometric Mouse: Variation 1, Scale A,* kids are challenged to wonder what it would be like to be a geometric mouse visiting a mouse house with 500 other geometric mice. To design a DIY tour for your brood, allow the kids to choose their own art cards and go to the youngest child's selections first.

The Hirshhorn's ArtLab (just off the Sculpture Garden) offers classes taught by artists and art educators. Children and their parents can drop in to hear Gallery Tales for Tots or participate in hands-on art projects inspired by work displayed in the galleries.

If you like this sight, you may also like the sculpture garden at the National Gallery of Art and Sculpture Garden (#36). Ask your kids if they can spot works by the same artists in both locations.

KEEP IN MIND
The Hirshhorn suggests connecting pieces with meaningful personal experiences. Picasso's *Woman with a Baby Carriage* might elicit a story about pushing your own baby. Although children are encouraged to get to know the art, please remind them that it's for the eyes, not the fingers.

EATS FOR KIDS When the Hirshhorn opened in 1974, detractors who didn't like the cylindrical architecture of the museum called it the Doughnut on the Mall. **On the Fly** food carts don't sell doughnuts, but they do carry tacos and hot dogs for carnivores and herbivores. These green-and-white carts are often in front of the Hirshhorn unless the skies or sales are dismal. For other options, *see* listings under the Castle (#65).

INTERNATIONAL SPY MUSEUM

I spy. You spy. Everyone spies here. Whether they're eavesdropping on siblings or snooping for hidden presents, youngsters just love to spy—and this museum takes the art of espionage to new levels for junior James Bonds, young Nancy Drews, and aspiring Spy Kids.

Did you know there are more spies in Washington than in any other city? Crowds of curious visitors walk through metal detectors and watch a short video on espionage before winding through the exhibits. Like little moles, kids can crawl through the museum's ductwork to peek through the vents. They can find larger-than-life-size silver flies on walls that transmit information to undisclosed locations.

Despite all the cool gadgetry that tempts kids to speed through too quickly in hot pursuit of adventure, take your time when you see the replica of James Bond's Aston Martin sports car. Just like in the films, gadgets galore pop out.

EATS FOR KIDS

A growling stomach attracts too much attention for a spy in hiding. Curb your appetite with a burger, a hot dog, or a made-to-order milk shake from the on-site **Shake Shack**. To avoid lunchtime crowds, cross the street to **Subway** (901 E St., tel. 202/737–3480).

KEEP IN MIND

Teens eager to put their sleuthing skills to work, can crack a safe, conduct a polygraph test, weigh evidence, and more courtesy of Operation Spy. This one-hour program gives participants aged 12 and older a chance to "feel, think, and act" like real intelligence officers. Operation Spy costs $15 per person (combination tickets with admission are available) and reservations, though not required, are recommended. The spies work in groups of about 15 with operations running about every 10 to 15 minutes. Also note: Everyone is required to exit the museum through the well-stocked gift shop.

 800 F St. NW.
Metro: Gallery Place/Chinatown

 $20, $15 children
age 7–11

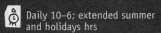 Daily 10–6; extended summer
and holidays hrs

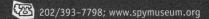 202/393-7798; www.spymuseum.org

 10 and up

Watch as people transform themselves into spies on videos that make Superman's telephone booth transition look way too simple. Through wardrobe changes, makeup, facial hair, and shoe inserts to make a person limp, a man and a woman morph into people their own close friends probably couldn't recognize.

While the museum offers clues and commentary on the capture of Robert Hanssen, Aldrich Ames, and other modern spies, a professional spy from the 12th century may draw just as much interest. In a huge glass cage, a life-size figure of a masked Ninja poses, representing the Japanese art of invisibility. Other tricks of the trade include cameras in buttons and homing pigeons, a pistol in a lipstick, a transmitting device in a tree stump, and a microphone wristwatch.

If you like this sight, you may also like the National Air and Space Museum (#42).

MAKE THE MOST OF YOUR TIME At peak times—spring and summer weekends, Thanksgiving, and Christmas—the museum recommends buying tickets through their website at least 48 hours in advance. The high-tech feel of this metallic-and-wood museum is particularly cool for preteens and teenagers. If you bring along a younger sibling, your child might not be only one who gets tired, as seating is limited and strollers aren't allowed in the museum (nor are food, beverages, or cameras).

KENILWORTH NATIONAL
AQUATIC GARDENS

Children like to run through this 12-acre national park devoted to aquatic plants. However, the best way to enjoy it is to walk quietly and pause often. Hear bullfrogs croak and birds chirp, search for turtles and frogs among platter-size leaves, gaze on exotic plants and water lilies reminiscent of a Monet painting. A clever game of "I Spy" might slow the kids down enough to savor the sanctuary's true pleasure—bird-watching. With redwing blackbirds, blue herons, and bald eagles there's plenty to see.

Ask your youngsters how cattails and yellow flag irises got their names or whether pickerelweeds and rose mallow shrubs (no relation to marshmallows) look as silly as they sound. Listen to the bullfrogs; then watch for turtles sunbathing and crayfish burrowing. The beaver dams are worth a look, too. Beavers like to dine on the water lilies, which is why the most expensive plants are close to the visitor center. Don't restrict yourselves to sight and sound, though: Let your other senses, like smell (tasting isn't recommended), guide you.

EATS FOR KIDS Alas, there's no food for humans here (only water), and there aren't any restaurants within walking distance of these gardens tucked away in a corner of Northeast Washington. Pack a big lunch and take advantage of the **picnic tables** near the ponds.

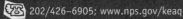 1550 Anacostia Ave. NE

 Daily 7–4

 Free

 2 and up

202/426–6905; www.nps.gov/keaq

If you are traveling with a toddler or preschooler, plan to spend at least 10 minutes in the visitor center, where they can attach pictures of the gardens' animals to a mural. For groups with older kids, the center is the place to pick up maps and activity booklets.

In winter, you can search for the shells of pond crustaceans left by birds and follow animal tracks. Do you think the bird got away, or did the fox eat last night? In spring, you may hunt for muskrat holes in the dikes or watch female dragonflies dip their tails in the water to lay eggs. Whatever the season, it's fun watching kids explore Kenilworth.

If you like this sight, you may also like the U.S. National Arboretum (#8).

MAKE THE MOST OF YOUR TIME
The best time to visit is between 8 AM and 11 AM, when day-bloomers are opening and night-bloomers have yet to close. Water lilies flower throughout the summer.

KEEP IN MIND Driving directions are tricky (when using a GPS, be sure to note the zip code: 20019). If you do get lost, you should know that locals refer to Kenilworth as "lily ponds." Keep a careful eye on children, especially preschoolers, while they search for aquatic life. Although the ponds are only 3 feet deep, the banks can be slick and there are no fences around them. The only barriers are those in the ponds, designed to protect the plants. And don't worry if your clothes get a little dirty. It's all part of the fun.

KENNEDY CENTER

The Kennedy Center looks like a place for adults in tuxedos and chic black dresses—and it is. But it's also a place that rolls out the red carpet for children. As the nation's performing arts center, it takes seriously its responsibility to make an eclectic calendar of top-notch shows accessible to many.

More than 100 family events in a wide range of genres are staged annually through the Center's Performances for Young Audiences program. Moreover, the National Symphony Orchestra, which is based here, puts on Kinderkonzerts and family concerts. Arrive 45 minutes early for most of its shows and your children can beat drums, blow into a tuba, or clang cymbals at the Orchestra's "Petting Zoo." Tots and their stuffed animal friends love the popular Teddy Bear Concerts where musicians play on tiny versions of their instruments—like the ones they used when they were little.

KEEP IN MIND

The 618-foot-long Grand Foyer is one of the world's largest rooms. If you could lay the Washington Monument on its side there, you'd still have about 3 inches to spare! Look up to see tons of crystal—literally. Each of the 18 chandeliers weighs one ton.

MAKE THE MOST OF YOUR TIME

Cue sheets for many children's performances are available online. Not only do the sheets provide background information on the performers and their art, they often give kids a list of things to look for when watching a show. The Center also offers sensory-friendly performances with adjusted sound levels and space for movement to make the theater a welcoming space for children with special needs and their families.

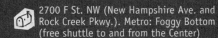

2700 F St. NW (New Hampshire Ave. and Rock Creek Pkwy.). Metro: Foggy Bottom (free shuttle to and from the Center)

202/467–4600 or 800/444–1324; www.kennedy-center.org

Free, children's performances free–$18

Daily 10 AM–midnight (or until last show lets out); box office M–Sa 10–9, Su 12–9

4 and up (depending on performance)

As part of the Performing Arts for Everyone Initiative, free one-hour performances are held nightly at 6 on the Millennium Stage (neither ticket nor reservation required). Many provide the perfect opportunity to introduce children to classical music or opera. In others, dancers, actors, storytellers, or magicians reach out to kids of all ages. Seats are generally plentiful, though kids often sit up front or on the steps, or they don't sit at all—they dance!

Even without seeing a performance, you can enjoy this six-theater memorial to President Kennedy. Pick up a "flag sheet" at the information desk, and visit the Hall of Nations and Hall of States, where the flags of more than 140 countries and all 50 states hang, the latter in order of admission to the union.

If you like this sight, you might also like the Washington National Cathedral (#5). You can see it from the Kennedy Center Roof Terrace.

EATS FOR KIDS For restaurants with a view, you can't beat the top of the Kennedy Center. The **KC Café** offers self-serve soup, sandwiches, pasta salads, and pizza overlooking the Potomac and Georgetown. The formal **Roof Terrace Restaurant** (tel. 202/416–8555) isn't appropriate for most kids, but it could be a great place to start the evening for older children with tickets to a play. Although prices at both the café and restaurant tend to be steep, the service is quick, ensuring that you get to the show on time!

LINCOLN MEMORIAL

Give your kids five, as in five dollars. Or give them a penny. Either way, they'll see a picture of the Lincoln Memorial. Then take them to see the real thing.

Children eager to show off newly acquired counting skills will find plenty to keep them busy here. Thirty-six Doric columns, representing the 36 states in the country at the time of Lincoln's death, surround the somber statue of the seated president. Above the frieze are the names of the 48 states of the union when the memorial was dedicated in 1922. (Alaska and Hawaii are noted by an inscription on the terrace leading up to the memorial.)

Older children may practice their oratorical skills by reciting two of Lincoln's great speeches—"The Second Inaugural Address" and "The Gettysburg Address"—which are carved on the north and south walls. Kids can even find the exact spot on the steps of the Lincoln Memorial where Martin Luther King Jr. gave his famous "I Have a Dream" speech in 1963 (look down for the engraving added in 2003).

EATS FOR KIDS A **refreshment stand** (French Dr., north side of Independence Ave. SW), located just a short walk from the memorial, serves sandwiches, french fries, chicken fingers, and the like.

 West end of Mall NW.
Metro: Foggy Bottom

 Free

 202/426-6841;
www.nps.gov/linc

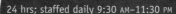 24 hrs; staffed daily 9:30 AM–11:30 PM

 3 and up

Also pay special attention to Lincoln's face and hands. They look particularly lifelike because they were based on castings done of Lincoln while he was in office. Those who know sign language might recognize that Lincoln's left hand is shaped like an "A" while his right hand looks like an "L." Although it's a myth that this was done on purpose, Daniel Chester French, the sculptor, happened to have a son who was deaf.

If you like this sight, there are plenty of other places where you can indulge a passion for the 16th president—including Ford's Theatre (#58), where he was shot, and the National Museum of Health and Medicine (#30), where the bullet that killed him is on display.

KEEP IN MIND
If your group feels too hot after walking up the steps, check out the gift shop. It may be tiny, but it is (thankfully) air-conditioned.

MAKE THE MOST OF YOUR TIME While many visitors look only at the front and inside of the monument, there is more to explore. On the lower level, to the left of the main stairs, is a mini-museum that was financed by pennies schoolchildren collected. An adjacent display chronicles the memorial's construction, and a video and photos depict famous demonstrations and speeches that have taken place here.

MADAME TUSSAUDS
WASHINGTON D.C.

Who says you won't see the President in Washington, D.C.?

Here, you can come face to face with all 44 of the men who have been POTUS (President of the United States). From 5'4" James Madison to 6'4" Abraham Lincoln, they're all ready for their close-up.

Though Madame Tussauds has been entertaining Europeans with its signature wax figures for 200-plus years, this Washington, D.C., showplace only opened in 2007.

More than 100 uncannily lifelike models form a virtual Who's Who of movies, music, sports, and, of course, politics featured in themed interactive exhibits. In Sports, kids can find out how much bigger they need to grow to measure up to Babe Ruth and Alex Ovechkin. In the Civil Rights Room, they can take a seat next to Rosa Parks on the bus. In Glamour, they can say hello to Disney star Selena Gomez while their parents are busy ogling Brad

MAKE THE MOST OF YOUR TIME

You can save on admission by buying tickets online or by flashing your American Automobile Association (AAA) card (even though you'll probably take the Metro). Some visitors may want to put those savings toward an "official portrait" of your family in the faux Oval Office.

EATS FOR KIDS Enchiladas and tacos aren't the only dishes for kids at **Austin Grill** (750 E St. NW, tel. 202/393–3776); they can order PB&J or carrots and celery sticks as well. **Clyde's of Gallery Place** (707 7th St. NW, tel. 202/349–3700) is part of the Clyde's restaurant group that has been serving D.C. diners for generations.

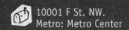 10001 F St. NW.
Metro: Metro Center

 202/942-7300; www.
madametussaudsdc.com

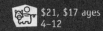 $21, $17 ages
4-12

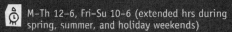 M-Th 12-6, Fri-Su 10-6 (extended hrs during
spring, summer, and holiday weekends)

 7 and up

Pitt or Julia Roberts. And in the Oval Office, your children can do more than sit behind the presidential desk—they can prop their feet up on it (assuming their legs are long enough!).

Speaking of feet, in Behind the Scenes, which focuses on how the wax figures are made, kids can compare their feet and hands with those of famous folk like Jennifer Lopez and Evander Holyfield. They can make a mold of their own hands, too.

After seeing so many celebs, your children may feel entitled to brag a bit. Well, they can tell more than their friends: At the museum's final stop, kids can reveal all to Katie Couric, while proud parents watch on a nearby TV monitor.

If you like this sight, you may also like the Newseum (#24), which gives kids another chance to appear on camera.

KEEP IN MIND Your kids might be wondering who Madame Marie Tussaud was. Born in France in 1761, a young Marie learned her skills from a physician. During the French Revolution, she was captured but managed to keep her head—and the death masks of guillotined nobles that she had collected. She fled to England, where these gruesome models became a touring exhibition. In addition to this attraction and the London original, there are eight more Madame Tussauds museums throughout the world.

MARTIN LUTHER KING JR. MEMORIAL

46

The United States has never had kings or queens, but we have had a "King."

This man—Martin Luther King Jr.—now stands tall among the presidents on the National Mall. At the dedication of his memorial on October 16, 2011, President Barak Obama said, "This is a day that would not be denied." The memorial opened 15 years after Congress approved it in 1996 and 82 years after the famed civil rights leader was born in 1929.

Located strategically between those commemorating Lincoln and Jefferson, the crescent-shape memorial sits on a 4-acre site on the curved bank of the Tidal Basin.

You enter via a walkway cut out of a huge bolder representing the Mountain of Despair, the symbolism of which is explained by King's words: "With this faith, we will be able to hew out of the mountain of despair a stone of hope." The centerpiece is a 28-foot-high statue of King, created by Lei Yixin. Fittingly, the Chinese sculptor first became acquainted with his subject's famous "I Have a Dream" speech at age 10 while visiting the Lincoln Memorial.

EATS FOR KIDS Like other memorials on the National Mall, this one doesn't serve food. Consider strolling over to the National Museum of American History (*see* #32) to see the famous lunch counter from a segregated restaurant where black college students staged a 1960 sit-in; then salute their actions by sitting anywhere you want at one of that museum's **cafés**.

1964 Independence Ave., SW, The Mall
Metro: Smithsonian

 Free

 Open 24 hrs; staffed daily 9:30 AM–
11:30 PM

 202/426–6841; www.nps.gov/mlkm

9 and up

Needless to say, the more your child knows about King, the more meaningful your visit will be. Without prior understanding of why he lived up to his name, many could be bored here.

Try to arrange your trip to coincide with ranger talks, which are given every two hours beginning at 10 AM daily. A book of quotations (available in the gift shop) will also help as the themes of democracy, justice, hope, and love are reflected through quotes on the south and north walls and on the Stone of Hope. These were gleaned from speeches, sermons, and writings penned by King from 1955 through 1968. But perhaps his most remarkable words are ones you won't see here: "I have a dream."

If you like this sight, walk over to the Lincoln Memorial (#48) where you can stand on the same step that King delivered his famous line from. It's marked by a plaque.

MAKE THE MOST OF YOUR TIME If your child has
questions, cross West Basin Drive to visit the park ranger station and gift shop. The ranger will give you a free brochure and Junior Ranger booklet for the National Mall. The gift shop sells books and a variety of quality keepsakes. This is also a good place for a break because the restrooms are well lit and tidier than most others at memorials.

KEEP IN MIND
On a sunny day, wear sun protection and sunglasses as there's no shade at this open memorial. Also, keep your eyes on little ones who may be tempted to wander. There's no barrier between the path around the Tidal Basin and the water.

MEDIEVAL TIMES DINNER & TOURNAMENT

45

Young ladies and lords have a regal time at this replica of a castle from the Middle Ages cast in the most modern of settings—a shopping mall.

Dine on a medieval-style four-course feast while valiant knights on horseback compete in games of skill and jousting during a live two-hour performance.

Like any gracious host and hostess, the king and princess greet each guest on arrival. Everyone receives a crown in a color that determines which of six knights you'll cheer for and where you'll dine in the 1,000-seat, color-coded arena. (If your child has a color preference, let the staff know.)

Some children may actually follow the show's plot, which involves the evil Herald from the North who tries to capture King Carlos' daughter Princess Catalina while horses dance to recorded, yet original, symphonic music. But for most boys and girls, the storyline is secondary to the action.

KEEP IN MIND

Medieval Times is in Arundel Mills Mall. To reach it, take I-95 north to exit 43A (Route 100 East), then exit 10A (Arundel Mills Blvd.). From the Baltimore–Washington Parkway, proceed to Arundel Mills Boulevard.

MAKE THE MOST OF YOUR TIME

Medieval Times encourages guests to arrive one hour early. This allows time for parents to park and kids to get crowned. Browse the on-site shop—or not—it's full of temptations like wooden swords, and costumes for squires and princesses. The Torture Chamber is small and definitely not for young children. But the $2 cover charge could be worth the price of admission for tweens and teen who may be so grossed out by the replica torture devices that getting grounded for a day would seem, in comparison, like a mild punishment.

 7000 Arundel Mills Circle, Hanover, MD
(Arundel Mills Mall)

 888/935-6878; www.
medievaltimes.com

 $57, $36 ages 4–12, under
4 (on laps) free; taxes and
gratuities extra

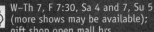 W–Th 7, F 7:30, Sa 4 and 7, Su 5
(more shows may be available);
gift shop open mall hrs

 4 and up

Everyone is encouraged to root for their knights, and the crowd becomes boisterous as the battle begins. Knights on and off horses compete to become the champion. Although the weapons aren't sharp, they still create sparks when they clash, and the stunts are real. With swords, axes, spears, shields, and even hand-to-hand combat, knights duke it out. (Because the action seems quite realistic—and takes place in semi-darkness—it may be too much for the timid.)

Notice the accuracy as the knights throw lances to one another while riding on horseback. They train by tossing water balloons back and forth! Maybe you'd be surprised to learn that some of the knights were recruited for their athleticism and originally didn't know how to ride at all. They start as squires and train for 8 to 12 months before becoming knighted by the king.

If you like this sight, you might also like riding horses at Rock Creek Park (#19). It's the only place to mount up in Washington, D.C.

EATS FOR KIDS Don't expect your young royals to eat daintily. They can't: As in the Middle Ages, diners don't use silverware. All four courses are finger food, except for the soup, which you drink out of the bowl. Everyone is served the same fare regardless of age or preference. So if your kids wouldn't like the creamy tomato bisque, garlic bread, chicken, spare ribs, and herb-basted potato, you might want to factor in a trip into the Arundel Mills Mall **food court** (tel. 410/540–5110; www.simon.com/mall/arundel-mills). Note that beverage choices are limited to Pepsi products, tea, and water.

MOUNT VERNON

How much does your child know about our first president? Chances are not as much as you did when you were a kid. The people at Mount Vernon want to change that. A visit here offers much more than a chance to see George Washington's elegant and stately mansion. At the Ford Orientation Center and the Donald W. Reynolds Museum and Education Center, visitors get to know the Washington who was not just a renowned soldier but also an entrepreneur, a stepfather . . . and a kid. After purchasing a ticket, start at the orientation center, which features Mount Vernon in Miniature. With a step up on the platform, even preschoolers can watch with everyone else as drawers open, windows open, and fireplaces glow in this exact replica of the mansion.

During the 30-minute house tour, interpreters talk about Washington's home, answer questions, and give you a sense of who the country's first president really was. Be sure to tell your children to look up at the ceiling in the first room to find pictures of farm tools. Upstairs, the beds may look small, but that's an optical illusion resulting from their being high

EATS FOR KIDS To protect Mount Vernon from damage and litter, food and beverages aren't permitted on the grounds; however, water fountains are located near the mansion and all restrooms. Popcorn (which George Washington ate), pizza (which he didn't), and more are available in the **food court pavilion** with indoor and outdoor seating in the Reynolds building. For a taste of Colonial life, head instead to the **Mount Vernon Inn** (tel. 703/780–0011) and sample Colonial Turkey Pye (turkey and mixed veggies topped with a homemade buttermilk biscuit) or peanut-and-chestnut soup. The inn also offers modern kid-friendly meals, like chicken fingers and hamburgers.

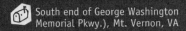

off the ground. The shortest mattress is 6'3", a tad longer than the general himself. Perhaps more interesting to kids than the house are a dozen meticulously restored outbuildings, including a major greenhouse, a kitchen, stables, and slave quarters.

The new Education Center is well worth the extra time. Sixteen galleries roughly follow a chronological view of Washington's life. Kids especially enjoy the animated cartoon of Washington's early years, Washington's false teeth, life-size images of Washington, and the movie in the First in War Gallery, where on-screen action is enhanced by falling snow, rumbling seats, and wafting fog.

For children who must touch everything, visit the Hands-on History room, where they can play games and dress up.

If you like Mount Vernon, you may also like the Washington Monument (#6).

KEEP IN MIND
The film *We Fight to be Free* in the Ford Orientation Center offers a wonderful overview of the estate and George Washington, but if your child is under six or afraid of loud noises, you won't want to stay past the first 15 minutes.

MAKE THE MOST OF YOUR TIME
There's so much to do, see, and learn that you could easily spend a day here and not get bored. Of course, lots of people know this—which explains why Mount Vernon is the most popular historic home in the country. Tourists pull up by the busload in spring and summer. To avoid the crowds, you could come late in the afternoon; just remember that the grounds close at 5. No matter when you arrive, pick up an Adventure Map to enhance your visit.

MYSTICS BASKETBALL

43

Kids don't need a wand or sorcerer's stone to enjoy the magic of the Mystics, Washington's popular WNBA team. Adults don't need a wad of money either. At a fraction of what it costs to watch the Wizards (Washington's NBA team) in action, you can catch a family-friendly Mystics game. Just like their male counterparts, the women's team fulfills children's hoop dreams at the Verizon Center: a 20,000-seat arena at the crossroads of Metro's red, green, and yellow lines.

Women have clearly come a long way since they first dribbled basketballs in 1892, a year after the game was invented and nearly three decades before they won the vote. People could have hardly imagined a women's professional basketball league back in the early 1890s, when female players wore floor-length dresses, even on the court. They gained more freedom in 1896, when they began playing in bloomers (loose-fitting trousers gathered at the knee). Now they, like men, dress for comfort and ease of motion, sweating through plenty of socks—around 960 all told!—each season.

MAKE THE MOST OF YOUR TIME

Gather a group of 20 or more and you not only qualify for discount tickets, you can have a message, such as "Happy Birthday" or "Congratulations," highlighted on the telescreen. You don't even need to plan far in advance. A day's notice (tel. 202/527–7518) will do!

EATS FOR KIDS If you don't feel like eating standard game fare at the Verizon Center, stroll under the gold–and–red arch to Chinatown. The noodle chef entertains folks as he stretches dough into strips of pasta from the front window of **Chinatown Express** (746 6th St. NW, tel. 202/638–0424). You can either order your noodles with beef, chicken, or seafood, or simply slurp them in a soup. **Tony Cheng's** (619 H St. NW, tel. 202/371–8669) offers barbecue on the first floor and a traditional menu upstairs.

601 F St. NW. Metro: Gallery Place/Chinatown

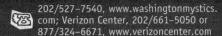 202/527-7540, www.washingtonmystics. com; Verizon Center, 202/661-5050 or 877/324-6671, www.verizoncenter.com

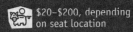 $20–$200, depending on seat location

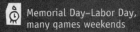 Memorial Day–Labor Day, many games weekends

 5 and up

During the game, a panda named Pax and 25 Mayhem dancers, ages 7 to 18, cheer on the players and spread high-fives through the crowd. Just think: Hundreds of kids try out for the Mayhem. During the game, other youngsters give out bangers (long balloons that when clapped together create a thunderous sound) that add to the excitement.

Need another reason to see the Mystics? It's easier to get tickets for their games than for those played by either the Wizards or the Verizon Center's other pro team, the puck-whacking Capitals of the NHL.

If you like the Mystics, you might also like another testament to the power of women—the National Museum of Women in the Arts (#27).

KEEP IN MIND If you ever come to see the Capitals (tel. 202/ 266-2350; capitals.nhl.com), you might want to visit the Hockey 101 booth, where team representatives answer your questions. For example, how many sticks do the players use? Some players may go through a couple per game, while others use one for a whole season. How do players sharpen their skates? They don't. The equipment manager sharpens them. If your kids are too young to ask questions, they might enjoy a hug from Slapshot, the Capitals' mascot.

NATIONAL AIR AND SPACE MUSEUM

There's a good reason why this place is the most popular museum in the U.S. and the second most popular on the planet: Kids adore it. The 22 galleries here tell the story of aviation and space from the earliest human attempts at flight. Suspended from the ceiling like plastic models in a child's room are dozens of vintage aircraft, including Charles Lindbergh's *Spirit of St. Louis,* the X-1 rocket plane in which Chuck Yeager broke the sound barrier, and the X-15, the fastest aircraft ever built.

Kids love walking through the backup model of the *Skylab* orbital workshop to see how astronauts live. At the How Things Fly gallery, they sit in a real Cessna 150 cockpit, "perform" experiments in midair, and see wind-tunnel demonstrations. An activity board at the gallery entrance lists times for family favorites such as paper airplane contests and demos by museum "Explainers" (high school and college students who encourage kids to participate). Over at the Explore the Universe exhibit, kids discover how past stargazers mapped the heavens with telescopes, cameras, and spectroscopes and learn what mysteries about our universe still remain.

MAKE THE MOST OF YOUR TIME Each year, a whopping 6 to 9 million visitors come here. To avoid the worst crowds, arrive early on a weekday morning—ideally in fall or winter. Tickets to IMAX films and planetarium shows sell out quickly, so buy them on arrival (or online in advance).

Independence Ave. at 6th St. SW.
Metro: L'Enfant Plaza

202/633-2214 or 202/633-1000 museum,
202/633-4629 or 877/932-4629 theater/
planetarium; airandspace.si.edu

 Free

 Daily 10–5:30

 3 and up

Don't let long lines deter you from seeing a show in the five story Lockheed Martin IMAX Theater. Films like *To Fly!* make you feel you've left the ground. Strollers aren't allowed at the movies, but little ones under age four may find the noise and larger-than-life images too frightening anyway.

For a look at the final frontier, check out the Albert Einstein Planetarium's five productions. In *One World One Sky: Big Bird's Adventure,* Big Bird and Elmo explore the night sky with Hu Hu Zhu, a Muppet from the Chinese co-production of *Sesame Street. The Stars Tonight,* for stargazers six and up, discusses what you can expect to see in the current sky.

Before you leave the museum, go to Milestones of Flight to touch the moon rock. It is one of only three on the planet that you can actually feel.

If you like this sight, you may also like the Steven F. Udvar-Hazy Center (#41).

KEEP IN MIND
On top of being crowded, this museum is huge (three blocks). Consider dressing your children in identical colors so that you can spot them easily. Also, review safety rules ahead of time, and point out what the security officers are wearing (white shirts, navy slacks, and hats) so your children know who to turn to if they get lost.

EATS FOR KIDS In the **food court**, grab a bite from familiar eateries like **McDonald's**, **Boston Market,** and **Donatos Pizza**. After lunch, go to the Observatory on the terrace outside the cafeteria. Looking through the 16-inch telescope, you can discover craters on the Moon, spots on the Sun (using safe solar filters), the phases of Venus and more. If you want a treat to take home, head to the tri-level gift shop, which sells flight-related merchandise like freeze-dried astronaut food.

NATIONAL AIR AND SPACE
MUSEUM'S STEVEN F. UDVAR-HAZY CENTER

41

Like its older, smaller sibling (the National Air and Space Museum on the Mall, *see #42*), the Steven F. Udvar-Hazy Center tells the story of aviation and space exploration. But this museum isn't divided into galleries. Instead, all manner of flying machines are displayed in huge hangars on three levels under a ceiling that's 10-stories high.

This gargantuan Smithsonian facility displays hundreds of aircraft, spacecrafts, rockets, satellites, and more, including a Concorde (the iconic, supersonic passenger jet), the fabled Lockheed SR-71 *Blackbird* (which in 1990 flew from Los Angeles to D.C. in slightly more than an hour), the *Enola Gay* (which in 1944 dropped the first atomic devices ever used in war on Japan), and the Space Shuttle *Discovery* (the longest-serving orbiter, which flew 39 times from 1984 through 2011, spending altogether 365 days in space).

When you enter, you'll be in the Boeing Aviation Hangar, with civil aviation to the left and military aviation to the right. Straight ahead you'll see *Discovery*.

KEEP IN MIND

Check out the Discovery Carts throughout the center. You might just get to try on replicas of $20,000 space gloves while younger children can play with astronaut dolls. You also might learn how astronauts take care of elimination issues (imagine oversized diapers).

MAKE THE MOST OF YOUR TIME

There's a $15 fee to park your car in the gigantic lot right in front of the museum. You really don't have any other options, so be prepared to pay up. The only way around it is to visit after 4 when parking is free. Other expenses might include an IMAX movie, a trip on a flight simulator, and a souvenir from the gift shop.

 14390 Air and Space Museum Pkwy., Chantilly, VA

 703/572-4118 or 202/633-1000; airandspace.si.edu

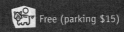 Free (parking $15)

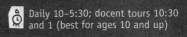 Daily 10-5:30; docent tours 10:30 and 1 (best for ages 10 and up)

 2 and up

The museum's wide aisles and cement floors are ideal for strollers, and the planes are big enough that parents of toddlers don't have to hoist them up on their shoulders to see. (As a matter of fact, signs throughout the museum let you know that adults can't hold kids on their shoulders for safety reasons.) Skywalks will take you nose-to-nose with the smaller aircraft suspended from the ceiling.

You can't miss the big stuff, but if you don't look carefully at the display cases, you might bypass some unexpected treasures, such as space toys, memorabilia from the days of Lindbergh-mania, personal items the astronauts carried, and a space-traveling spider named Anita.

Before you leave, make sure you go to the Observation Tower. Here you can see planes taking off and landing at nearby Dulles International Airport and get a panoramic view of Northern Virginia.

If you like this sight, you may also like the National Air and Space Museum (#42) and the College Park Aviation Museum (#63).

EATS FOR KIDS On-site choices here are limited to a **McDonald's** and a **McCafé**. For more options, take off down Route 50, where you can find local chain restaurants such as **Anita's** (13921 Lee Jackson Hwy., tel. 703/378-1717), with mini-tacos for kids, and national chains, such as **Bob Evans** (14050 Thunderbolt Pl., tel. 703/834-0511), where spaghetti is popular at lunch. Note that if you leave the center you can't reenter without paying for parking again, so you may want to plan your visit so it doesn't conflict with lunch or snack time.

NATIONAL AQUARIUM

The basement of the Department of Commerce building is a strange address for a tourist attraction, but that's where you'll find the nation's oldest public aquarium, which was established in the 1870s.

Unlike more modern aquariums, this one is compact enough that you can circle through in about 20 minutes (twice as long if you read all the signs). The small size is a big plus for parents of little tykes. Aisles are wide enough for double strollers, and the aquarium isn't generally crowded. Nevertheless, more than 250 species and 1,500 specimens of aquatic life, including American alligators, spiny lobsters, venomous lionfish, clownfish, flesh-chomping piranhas, and their seaworthy mates swim here. Animals live in traditional rectangular tanks.

The aquarium features habitats that represent the National Marine Sanctuaries stretching from the Florida Keys to Fagatele Bay in American Samoa. Freshwater tanks focus on familiar friends such as turtles and newts, but there are a few unfamiliar fish, too. Take the boneytail chub: One of the rarest fish in the Colorado River, the chub is close to

MAKE THE MOST OF YOUR TIME If the National Aquarium whets your appetite for fish, visit the glitzier **National Aquarium** (Pier 3, tel. 410/576–3800; www.aqua.org) in Baltimore. This sister site, an hour's drive from D.C. off-peak, is Maryland's top tourist attraction. Just be warned: It's more expensive—and more crowded—than Washington's version.

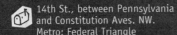14th St., between Pennsylvania and Constitution Aves. NW.
Metro: Federal Triangle

202/482-2825; www.aqua.org

$10 ages 12 and up, $5 ages 3–11

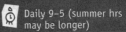Daily 9–5 (summer hrs may be longer)

1–7

extinction because so many dams were built. It grows up to about 2 feet and may live more than 40 years.

Free hands-on programs aimed at teaching tots more about marine life run the first and third Friday of each month at 10 AM. Special themed events for all ages are also held throughout the year.

On Shark Day you can watch a shark dissection. On Reptile Day, herpetologists (reptile experts) rave about these cold-blooded vertebrates and offer interesting sound "bites." Did you know, for instance, that an American alligator has 80 cone-shaped teeth that fall out twice a year until the 'gator stops growing? That must keep the tooth fairy—or shall we say tooth mermaid—busy!

If you like this sight, you may also like the National Zoo (#25).

KEEP IN MIND You can't buy a pet piranha, but the aquarium's spacious gift shop does sell necklaces with shark's teeth, T-shirts, stuffed sea-horses, and other marine-themed treasures.

EATS FOR KIDS Sharks are fed at 2 on Monday, Wednesday, and Saturday. Piranhas are fed at 2 on Tuesday, Thursday, and Sunday. Alligators are fed at 2 on Friday. People, on the other hand, can catch a bite any time at food courts in the lower level of the **Ronald Reagan Building** (1300 Pennsylvania Ave. NW, tel. 202/312–1300). On a pleasant day, you could also walk over to the top level of the **Shops** (see the White House #2).

NATIONAL ARCHIVES

W here does your family keep its important papers? Our nation's most precious documents are housed at the National Archives.

Here you can see the Declaration of Independence, the Constitution, and the Bill of Rights. If you think about it, it's rather extraordinary that our country puts these irreplaceable papers on display, allowing throngs of visitors to peer through protective glass for a glimpse of history. In case you're wondering, that glass is equipped with filters and filled with argon gas (it's colorless, odorless, and tasteless) to shield the documents from light and air, which fade and deteriorate both ink and paper.

One of the most frequent questions kids ask about the National Archives concerns the 2004 award-winning movie *National Treasure,* starring Nicholas Cage. (The blockbuster wasn't filmed inside the building but it does feature some shots of the exterior.) In the movie, Cage's character steals the Declaration of Independence and finds a map on the

EATS FOR KIDS

If your child is hungry for more than knowledge, the on-site **Farmers Market Café** sells hot and cold sandwiches, snacks, and fresh fruit on weekdays. Its walls are lined with vintage agricultural posters from the archive's collection that encourage healthful eating.

MAKE THE MOST OF YOUR TIME

Unless you arrive on a blustery February day, be prepared to stand in line for at least 30 minutes. Make the most of this downtime by calling 202/357–6829 for an audio introduction to the Charters of Freedom and codes for discounts at the Archives Gift Shop, where you can buy clear copies of the documents. While waiting outside, ask kids to count the columns (there are 72). While waiting to see the big three documents (the Declaration, Constitution, and Bill of Rights), ask them to find three famous founders in the paintings—Thomas Jefferson, Benjamin Franklin, and George Washington.

back. If you could see the flipside of the original, you'd notice there is no such map; however, there is writing. It reads, "Original Declaration of Independence, dated 4th July 1776," and it appears upside down on the bottom of the document. Other objects in the archive's vast collection that may interest kids include a letter from seventh-grader Andy Smith asking President Reagan for federal funds to clean up a disaster area—his room.

As for the building itself, you might notice a similarity between it and the west wing of the National Gallery of Art and Sculpture Garden (*see* #36), the Thomas Jefferson Memorial (*see* #13), or the DAR Museum (*see* #61). John Russell Pope designed them all in a neoclassical-revival style.

If you like this sight, you might also like seeing the signatures of the signers of the Declaration carved into a stone wall at Constitution Gardens, near the Vietnam Veterans Memorial (#7).

KEEP IN MIND The Declaration wasn't always stored safely behind glass at the National Archives for millions of people to view. It has had many homes, including government offices, the interiors of safes, and other public displays. Wagons, ships, a Pullman sleeper, and an armored vehicle have transported this priceless document.

NATIONAL BUILDING MUSEUM

The Big Bad Wolf won't blow this house down! More than 15 million bricks make up the building, designed by Civil War veteran Montgomery Meigs and constructed between 1882 and 1887. Its scale will awe budding builders and aspiring architects. The Great Hall, where many inaugural balls were held, is 15-stories tall and as long as a football field. Eight 75-foot Corinthian columns are among the world's largest—and although they look like real stone, each is comprised of 70,000 bricks covered with plaster and marbleized.

The Building Zone is a magnet for kids who have transitioned from tearing down block towers to erecting their own. Designed for children two to six, the Zone has a dress-up section with hard hats, tool belts, and goggles for children who want to look like Bob the Builder. On weekends, they (and you) can learn how bridges work and how buildings, for the most part, manage to stay in one piece.

In the Washington: Symbol and City exhibit, children can handle plastic models of the Capitol, White House, Washington Monument, and Lincoln Memorial. In Play Work Build,

MAKE THE MOST OF YOUR TIME Borrow a tool kit for $5 at the information desk. "Patterns: Here, There, and Everywhere" (aimed at kids three to seven) has stamps, rubbings, and games for learning about brick patterns; "Eye Spy: What Can you Find With Your Little Eye?" (for the 7 to 10 set) includes jigsaw puzzles and create your own postcards; while "Constructor Detector" (targeted at tweens) includes a scavenger hunt and supplies to create a pattern that you can take home as a souvenir.

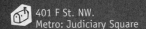
401 F St. NW.
Metro: Judiciary Square

202/272-2448; www.nbm.org

$8, $5 ages 3-17
(students need IDs),
$3 ages 3 and up for
Building Zone only

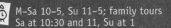
M-Sa 10-5, Su 11-5; family tours
Sa at 10:30 and 11, Su at 1

2 and up

adults may get a kick out of seeing some of the toys from their childhood, but most kids would rather build with the huge blue molded-foam blocks.

Special exhibits, which change as often as five times per year, all focus on the people, processes, or materials that create buildings and other "places." Recent ones have explored the art of Lego building, parking garages, and elevators, escalators, and moving sidewalks.

Every day the museum has other drop-in activities, most of which are free.

If you like this sight, you may also like Washington National Cathedral (#5). It's the sixth largest cathedral in the world and took less than a century to construct.

EATS FOR KIDS When appetites build, visit **FireHook Bakery and Coffee House** (tel. 202/628-0906) inside the museum for handcrafted and prepackaged sandwiches, salads, and desserts. Eat in or take your lunch out to the benches across the street at the National Law Enforcement Officers Memorial.

KEEP IN MIND Extensive school programs (also available to other groups, like scout troops) complement curricula in social studies, science, art, math, and history. Under the guidance of the museum's educators, students may plan an imaginary town, build model bridges, or assemble an 8' x 11' house from the ground up with foundations, wall frames, and trusses. Most programs cost a dollar or two per student. For information, call the museum's education department. Check out the museum store, known as one of the best such shops in D.C., for take-home building supplies.

NATIONAL CAPITAL TROLLEY MUSEUM

What small child doesn't love trains? And what small child who loves trains doesn't love trolleys? You can test this hypothesis here with a combination trolley trip and museum visit. The former, a 20-minute voyage, covers 1 mile of track through a wooded area. Often, passengers see deer, fox, rabbits, and groundhogs, but kids are usually content just watching the trolley operate.

The matching museum reopened in a new building in 2010. With a boost, even the smallest child can crank a handle to send a model trolley whizzing around in a case depicting Connecticut Avenue in the early 1930s. Older kids and parents can learn the parts of a trolley and the history of D.C. trolleys through interactive computers.

Also called streetcars, trolleys were introduced here by Lincoln's administration to accommodate the influx of people during the Civil War. Early ones were drawn by horses. These were replaced by cable cars and, ultimately, by electric cars, which skimmed

MAKE THE MOST OF YOUR TIME

Your trolley ticket makes a good souvenir. Each conductor uses a hole punch with a different shape—perhaps a star or zigzag. When the trolleys were in use, the holes helped identify conductors in case a passenger complained.

EATS FOR KIDS Food and drink aren't allowed in the museum or on the cars. But about three minutes away at the Layhill Shopping Center (Layhill and Bel Pre Rds.) you'll find Italian fare and video games at **Sole d' Italia** (tel. 301/598–6660), Chinese dishes at **Lee's Kitchen** (tel. 301/598–4810), plus familiar fast food at **McDonald's** and **Subway**.

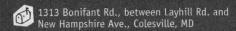 1313 Bonifant Rd., between Layhill Rd. and
New Hampshire Ave., Colesville, MD

 $7, $5 children 2–17

 Jan–Dec, Sa–Su 12–5; also mid-
Mar–mid-May, mid-June–mid-Aug
and Oct mid-Nov, Th–F 10–2

 301/384–6088; www.dctrolley.org

2–7 and all train lovers

quickly and smoothly along the tracks. The last Washington trolleys ran during the Kennedy administration. In fact, you might be riding in one of these last cars or in one from another country. The museum's collection includes a dozen, which are all brought out on the third Sunday in April for the Cavalcade of Cars and again on the third Sunday in September for the Fall Open House. Both events also feature other attractions, such as a barbershop quartet. During December's Holly Trolleyfest, Santa greets children during the ride.

Trolley memorabilia, *Thomas the Tank Engine* books, and other train-related merchandise are available in the shop. A free Little Folks Guide to the Trolley Museum handout and the trolley tickets themselves make nice mementos that can be used to play trolley at home.

If you like this museum, you might also like the College Park Aviation Museum (#63), a facility devoted to air transportation.

KEEP IN MIND The biggest trolley trick for parents of toddlers is keeping them safely seated during the short ride. Luckily, the trolley makes one stop en route, when kids can get up and walk around. This is also when enthusiastic volunteers give brief trolley talks and answer questions. Often some of the older passengers will remember riding the trolley when they were kids.

NATIONAL GALLERY OF ART
AND SCULPTURE GARDEN

Some think it looks like a bird, others a plane, but most agree that the Alexander Calder mobile soaring overhead in this museum's East Building atrium is super. Looming as large as a small aircraft, it's just one of the works that fascinates kids here. The art museum (one of the world's most visited) is made up of two very different buildings and a sculpture garden. The airy and spacious East Building's modern art—by Picasso, Matisse, Miró, and others—appeals to children, as does the exterior of the I. M. Pei–designed trapezoidal structure. In fact, since its 1978 opening, the bladelike southwest corner has been darkened and polished smooth by thousands of hands irresistibly drawn to touch it.

In the neoclassical West Building, more than 100 galleries contain pieces created prior to the 20th century. Though art lovers could easily spend all day here, most little tykes only last about an hour. (Strollers are available at both buildings' entrances.) Students of architecture may notice that the West Building's dome shape resembles the Jefferson

MAKE THE MOST OF YOUR TIME Free weekend Family Workshops (registration required; call up to three weeks in advance) include tours and activities. If you'd rather go it alone, start in the Information Room in the West Building to preview works by computer and pick up a free audio tour.

4th St. and Constitution Ave. NW, East Bldg.;
6th and Constitution Ave. NW, West Bldg.
Metro: Judiciary Square, Archives, Smithsonian

 Free

 M–Sa 10–5, Su 11–6

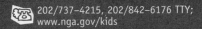
202/737–4215, 202/842–6176 TTY;
www.nga.gov/kids

 4 and up

Memorial. That makes sense because they were both designed by John Russell Pope and opened in the early 1940s.

Even tiny tots enjoy the sculpture garden. The massive *Spider* by Louise Bourgeois is large enough to frighten the bravest Miss Muffet. The rabbit *Thinker on a Rock* by Barry Flanagan can promote a discussion about other famous rabbits. Ask your child, "What do you suppose it's thinking about?" The only sculpture kids (or adults) can touch is Scott Burton's *Six-Part Seating,* with its polished granite chairs. Still, the meandering paths reveal unexpected treasures, such as Roxy Paine's *Graft* tree, Roy Lichtenstein's *House I,* or Claes Oldenburg and Coosje van Bruggen's mammoth *Typewriter Eraser, Scale X,* which looks foreign to computer-age kids. Ask yours to guess what it is.

If your family likes this sight, they may also like the Phillips Collection (#21).

KEEP IN MIND

When it's too cold to enjoy the sculpture garden, toddlers might be intrigued by *Multiverse,* the light sculpture by Leo Villareal in the Concourse walkway connecting the East and West buildings. For older kids, there's more to do here in winter than observe artwork. Ice-skating is offered mid-March through mid-November, weather permitting.

NATIONAL GEOGRAPHIC MUSEUM

35

The National Geographic Society's famous yellow-bordered magazine—found in doctors' offices, family rooms, and attics nationwide—isn't exactly for kids. Yet the Society's museum brings the planet's wonders closer, proving in the process that it is indeed a small world after all.

Exhibits rotate here just as the moon and Earth do, and the subject matter varies. Past visitors have investigated Animal Grossology (imagine gassy cows and blood-sucking leeches used after surgery), watched the *March of the Penguins* movie complete with a live appearance from these endearingly awkward birds, and studied King Tut's mummified remains. One exhibit about what scientists have learned from "Crittercams" (data-collecting devices worn by the animals) had kids crawling through a tunnel and popping up in a bubble to come face-to-face with a penguin outfitted with a working Crittercam.

KEEP IN MIND

Through magazines, TV, radio, maps, books, CD-ROMs, and the Internet, the National Geographic Society brings the world to more than 300 million people worldwide. You'll find many of the Society's publications in the gift shop, including *National Geographic Kids*, the magazine for 6- to 14-year-olds.

MAKE THE MOST OF YOUR TIME

The good news is that the exhibits here are well-researched, visually engaging, and, when family-oriented, very fun. The bad news is that there's a chance that the current exhibits might not be appropriate for all ages. Exhibits change about every three to six months, so check the website or call before you visit.

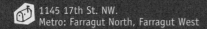 1145 17th St. NW.
Metro: Farragut North, Farragut West

 202/857-7588;
www.ngmuseum.org

 $8; $4 children 5–12

 Daily 10–6

 5 and up

Regardless of what is on display when you come, kids can ham it up and see their faces displayed on the cover of *National Geographic*. Postcard-size pictures ($5) can be made at In the Picture, where they can choose their own backgrounds from among a dozen scenes, including tulips outside the White House, the Great Wall of China, Mount Everest, or even the moon. Other props, like furry panda bears, tigers, or gorillas, complete the picture.

You can walk outside the museum's portico and peer through the glass 365 days of the year, 24 hours a day, to see relief maps created with satellite imagery as well as artifacts from past expeditions. You can also watch and listen to the National Geographic channel or check out the electronic ticker tape, which, not unexpectedly, tells about the latest expeditions, adventures, and discoveries in science and geography.

If you like this sight, you may also like the Newseum (#24).

EATS FOR KIDS In a neighborhood catering to businesspeople, you won't find high chairs, but you will find reasonable prices. In addition to a nearby **Quiznos** , **Potbelly**, and **Subway** , the self-service **California Grill** (1720 M St. NW, tel. 202/463–4200) sells a mix of cuisines, including Mexican, Greek and American, while the **Mudd House** (1724 M St. NW, tel. 202/822–8455) offers a place for parents to sip specialty coffees as kids warm up with hot chocolate. If you get take-out, eat in the shady courtyard behind the museum. In the spring, you might even see ducks in the little pond.

NATIONAL HARBOR

This waterfront destination with its hotels, restaurants, and shops has long been popular among convention attendees. But since the December 2012 debut of the National Children's Museum it has become a hit with kids as well. Designated by Congress, the 18,000-square-foot museum focuses on six topics: the environment, civic engagement, the arts, health, world cultures, and play. Big Bird and his pals welcome toddlers in the Three & Under Gallery, and the facility as a whole is mostly geared toward children who haven't yet reached the tween stage. Beyond the museum, an assortment of the other Harbor amusements beckons kids.

Take a picture (everyone else does) of your brood giving high-fives to a hand more than 100 times larger than their own, sliding down a huge leg, or sitting in a monstrous mouth and living to tell about it. Better yet, join in and climb all over *The Awakening,* the immense statue of a man who is half-buried in the ground. Transplanted from D.C.'s East Potomac Park, J. Seward Johnson's artwork reminds some kids of dad when he's waking up. Others

EATS FOR KIDS Kid-friendly food is easy to find because almost all of the two dozen restaurants in the Harbor have children's menus. One of the few eateries without waiter service, **Elevation Burger** (108 Waterfront St., tel. 301/749–4014) is known for its grass-fed organic beef. **McCormick & Schmick's** (145 National Plaza, tel. 301/567–6224) is part of a national chain that is typical here.

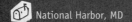

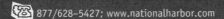

think he looks like a monster. Directly in front of *The Awakening,* Peeps & Company (150 National Plaza, tel. 301/749–5791; www.justborn.com) sells their signature mushy marshmallow Easter treats and other candies.

Fireworks, free movies, water taxis to D.C., and proximity to Mount Vernon (*see* #44) add to National Harbor's appeal in the summer, but winter might be the best time to visit. From mid-November through the first week in January, the Gaylord Hotel (201 Waterfront St., tel. 301/965–2000; www.gaylordhotels.com) hosts a winter wonderland called ICE! Sculptors hand-carve winter scenes that vary each year. Despite the 9° temperature inside (parkas given out at the door help ease the chill), many kids think it's quite nice or, shall we say, quite ice!

If you like this sight, you may also like Six Flags America (#16), another attraction in Prince George's County

MAKE THE MOST OF YOUR TIME
National Harbor isn't near D.C. attractions or a Metro rail station, and parking can be just as expensive here as it is downtown—or more so as there is no free parking even on Sunday.

KEEP IN MIND At the new **National Children's Museum** (open daily 10–5, 10–7 in summer; tel. 301/392–2400; www.ncm.museum) a $10 admission charge applies to every visitor over the age of one. If you are already a member of your hometown children's museum, ask if reciprocal benefits will allow you to get in free. Note that the museum's indoor space will be complemented by an "outdoor experience" that is slated to open late spring 2013.

NATIONAL MUSEUM OF AFRICAN ART

Children and adults aren't surprised to see some of the art at this museum because it's what people think of as typically "African." Beaded works, carvings, masks, and headdresses personifying characters or animals: you get the picture.

But there many are unexpected elements as well because the collection is a compelling mix of traditional and contemporary. Revolving exhibits illustrate the diversity of African art and crafts from the 55 countries comprising the continent, which is about three times as large as the United States.

Situated below a rooftop garden, 96% of this museum is underground, making it a nice outing for a rainy day. Depending on what's on display, you may see sculptures, textiles, photographs, archaeological artifacts, or modern art. To help in your exploration, consider counting the number of masks, comparing the textiles to the fabric in your own clothes, or looking for animals from an A-to-Z angle (antelopes, birds, crocodiles, dogs, elephants,

KEEP IN MIND

The gift shop, like all Smithsonian stores, doesn't charge any sales tax. Chances are you'll come across some cool items inside, including animals made from beads, wood, and even old soda cans. You might find chocolate bars from Ghana as well.

EATS FOR KIDS You can pick up fresh fruit, bread, and more on Friday, June through September, at the **Farmers Market** in the parking lot outside the Department of Agriculture (12th St. and Independence Ave.). The National Air and Space Museum, the National Museum of Natural History, the National Museum of the American Indian, and the National Museum of American History all have on-site restaurants (*see individual listings*).

 950 Independence Ave. SW.
Metro: Smithsonian

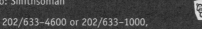 202/633-4600 or 202/633-1000,
202/633-5285
TTY; www.nmafa.si.edu

 Free

 Daily 10–5:30

 5 and up

fish, hyenas, and so on until you reach zebras). If your kids are inspired to create their own art, be sure to visit the Discovery Room where there's always paper and pencils available. Take your pictures home or put them in a box and a museum staffer will hang them up in the room for other visitors to enjoy.

The museum hosts storytelling sessions, during which folktales are frequently combined with music and dance to bring legends from the continent to life. And, in true African tradition, the audience regularly chimes in. On weekends, crafts for kids reflect the art and the seasons. As opposed to some other local museums, where craft sessions are aimed squarely at little tykes, this one has hands-on activities—like weaving baskets or painting gourds with African motifs—that are perfect for teens.

If you like this sight, you may also like the National Museum of Women in the Arts (#27).

MAKE THE MOST OF YOUR TIME To expand
your children's global view even further, walk about 100 paces west through
the Enid A. Haupt Garden or open the door at the end of the Walt Disney-
Tishman African gallery, and you'll be in the Sackler Gallery (see #17), which is
connected to the Freer Gallery of Art. Their emphasis is on another continent
altogether: Asia.

NATIONAL MUSEUM OF
AMERICAN HISTORY

Oh say, can you see the flag that inspired "The Star-Spangled Banner," Kermit the Frog, an original teddy bear from 1903, and inaugural gowns worn by famous first ladies? Yes, and you can see lots more classic American memorabilia, too.

If your kids love anything with wheels (or you happen to be obsessed with heavy equipment and old cars), begin your visit on the first floor. Exhibits there emphasize the history of science and technology and include farm machines, antique automobiles, plus a 260-ton steam locomotive. America on the Move starts in 1856 as the railroad comes to a California town and ends in 1999 in Los Angeles (the "Ellis Island of the end of the 20th century") as pilgrims arrive from other countries daily. Maybe your children will follow the 14 historical settings in chronological order, but chances are they'll zip through pointing out the 1939 Dodge school bus painted "double deep" orange; the toy ride-in car; and the 1955 station wagon with wood paneling. Look for "Bud," the official mascot of the exhibit. His signs are designed to stimulate family discussion.

KEEP IN MIND

This museum is undergoing renovations until 2015, but don't let that deter you. Kids can still learn a lot by walking around or even just sitting. Ask at the information desk when you can join a "sit-in," a theatrical performance about the 1960 protest at a "whites only" lunch counter in Greensboro, N.C.

MAKE THE MOST OF YOUR TIME

If you bring a purse or other bag with you, allow a little extra time for security. If you enter from the Mall, you might walk right past the welcome area. It's on the right. If you're looking for the Touch of History carts, they could be anywhere. But once you find one, the volunteer manning it can tell you where to find another. Cart activities vary depending on the exhibits. If you have a tween or teen with you, be sure to check out the Apple Macintosh computer in the American Stories exhibit.

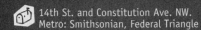
 14th St. and Constitution Ave. NW.
Metro: Smithsonian, Federal Triangle

 Free

 Daily 10–5:30

 2 and up

202/633-1000; www.
americanhistory.si.edu

The second floor, devoted to American lives and ideals, has other must see exhibits. Within These Walls follows five families who lived at 16 Elm Street in Ipswich, Massachusetts, from the mid-1760s through 1945. (Their actual house, partially reconstructed here, qualifies as the museum's single largest artifact). American Stories, meanwhile, retells the nation's tale through iconic items ranging from a fragment of Plymouth Rock to Dorothy's ruby slippers.

On the third floor, young fashionistas can admire the First Ladies' gowns. Those ladies' husbands warrant their own exhibit, The American Presidency: A Glorious Burden. Pint-sized politicos can peruse a large assortment of artifacts associated with presidents and "vote" for their favorite Commander in Chief.

If you like this sight, you may also like the National Museum of Natural History (#29), next door.

EATS FOR KIDS If your kids scream for ice cream, visit the museum's **Constitution Café** and ice cream bar (on the first floor, Constitution Ave. entrance) for an Italian treat. At the **Stars and Stripes Café** on the lower level, you can count on all-American options like barbeque, sandwiches, and salads. Occasionally the chefs will celebrate occasions such as Hispanic Heritage Month by adding tacos to the menu. When the weather is good, grab a hot dog from the **food carts** and picnic outside.

NATIONAL MUSEUM OF
THE AMERICAN INDIAN

Your introduction to Native American life and indeed U.S. history begins before you enter this Smithsonian museum, which opened in 2004. Plants that were indigenous to the area prior to the arrival of European settlers grow in an upland hardwood forest, lowland freshwater wetlands, and a meadow. Crops known as the "three sisters"—corn, beans, and squash—will also grow. Cascading water represents purification and a nurturing spirit. Even the building's Kasota limestone–clad forms reflect the wearing by wind and water over time.

As you step inside, listen to the words issuing out of the Welcome Wall: They come from languages spoken by Native people from the northern tip of the Arctic to the southern tip of South America. Then feel the cool copper bands woven into a wall surrounding the atrium, representing traditions of textiles and basketry.

During daily programs American Indians host weaving, boat building, dancing, and drumming demonstrations in the spacious Potomac Atrium. No matter what day you visit,

EATS FOR KIDS Watch salmon being cooked over a fire pit built into the floor of the museum's **Mitsitam Native Foods Café** (Mitsitam means "Let's Eat" in the language of the Delaware and Piscataway). If your kids don't care for salmon, choose from foods native to five geographic regions: Northern Woodlands, South America, Northwest Coast, Meso-American, and the Great Plains. Whatever regional cuisine you select, try to get a seat at the window where it looks as if the water outside disappears under your feet.

4th St. and Independence Ave. SW.
Metro: Federal Center SW/L'Enfant Plaza,
Maryland Ave. exit

 Free

 Daily 10–5:30

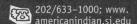
202/633-1000; www.
americanindian.si.edu

 2 and up

look at the "light show" reflected from the prism window. When the sun is at its peak, from 11 AM to 2 PM, the sun's beams and refractions dance across the floors and walls.

Also check out the floor-to-ceiling cases along the walls of the Window on Collections exhibits. Challenge your child to find the Inupiat school of fish carved from ivory, or the Assiniboine and Sioux dolls that are dressed in full regalia and made from buffalo hide.

Displays and demos aside, one of the best things about the museum is the way it busts cultural myths. You've heard of cowboys and Indians. Well, some Native Americans were and are cowboys and cowgirls, too. They still ranch and entertain folks with their rodeo skills. Even children who have studied American Indians may be surprised to learn that more died from diseases brought from European settlers than from wars.

If like this sight, you may also like the planetarium shows at Rock Creek Park (#19) that touch on Native American legends about the stars.

MAKE THE MOST OF YOUR TIME
Who We Are, a 13-minute presentation on the fourth floor, is a great introduction to contemporary Native life. But if your children cover their ears during thunderstorms, it might be wise to skip it.

KEEP IN MIND Build an igloo, weave a gigantic basket, and decide for yourself which is the coolest mode of transportation—skateboards or snowshoes—in the spacious imagiNATIONS activity center, open daily. If you'd like a more permanent memento of your visit, two museum stores carry an impressive array of books for children about Native American life plus authentic Native crafts at reasonable prices.

NATIONAL MUSEUM OF
HEALTH AND MEDICINE

There's much to make everyone grateful for modern medicine at this museum depicting the fight against injury and disease. Yet whether it's cool or creepy depends on your perspective. Because some exhibits are fairly graphic, it will be perfect for those fond of the word "gross" but may be unsuitable for the squeamish.

The museum, which started on a desktop (the old-fashioned, wooden kind) in 1862, has occupied several locations in the Washington area. Its latest move was in 2011 from Walter Reed Army Medical Center in Washington, D.C. to a new space 5 miles away in the Fort Detrick/Forest Glen Annex in Silver Spring, Maryland. One thing hasn't changed, though: It's still full of bizarre stuff and stories.

During the Battle of Gettysburg, for instance, a 12-pound cannonball splintered the right leg of Civil War General Daniel E. Sickles. After it was amputated, he sent the leg to the museum (then known as the Army Medical Museum)—and it remains on display, along

KEEP IN MIND
The nearest Metro is too far away for walking, but on-site parking is plentiful and free—as are the programs. The museum also sponsors free lectures at the Silver Spring Civic Building (1 Veteran's Pl., near the Silver Spring metro), usually on the last Tuesday night of the month.

MAKE THE MOST OF YOUR TIME
Docents lead tours of the museum on the second and fourth Saturday of every month at 10:30. These last 1–1½ hours and are recommended for ages 11 and up. Many docents bring out plastinated organs for you to feel. To keep *your* organs healthy, they share a tip unknown to Civil War physicians, who spread a lot of germs: Wash your hands!

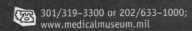 2500 Linden La., Silver Spring, MD

 Free

 Daily 10–5:30

 301/319–3300 or 202/633–1000;
www.medicalmuseum.mil

9 and up

with a picture of the general as an amputee. Incidentally, the eccentric Sickles used to visit his leg and would sometimes bring friends to see it.

Additional icky bits you can view include a brain still attached to a spinal cord, a leg infected with elephantiasis, and loads of body parts. Some organs are "plastinated" (preserved in plastic so they can be touched) and injected with blue and red dyes so arteries can be distinguished from veins. All are real.

At other exhibits, your children can learn about the evolution of the microscope, discover the development of the human embryo, see the human body from a 3-D perspective, and look at early medical instruments used in skull surgery. But the most famous object on display is the bullet that killed President Lincoln (*see* Ford's Theatre #58).

If you like this sight, you may also appreciate the medicinal plants at the United States Botanic Garden (#11).

EATS FOR KIDS If you still have an appetite, **Armands Pizza** (1909 Seminary Rd., tel. 301/588–3400) is less than a mile away. Its deep-dish Chicago-style pies are only available in D.C., Delaware, and Maryland. Two miles away in downtown Silver Spring, area favorites **Lebanese Taverna Café** (933 Ellsworth Dr., tel. 301/588–1192) and **CakeLove** (8512 Fenton St., tel. 301/565–2253) are situated near national chain restaurants, including **Austin Grill**, **Baja Fresh**, and **Panera Bread**.

Say hello to Henry, one of the largest elephants ever found. The taxidermist's dream come true has greeted generations of kids in the rotunda of this huge Smithsonian museum, which is dedicated to natural wonders of the world, both big and small.

In the popular first-floor Dinosaur Hall fossilized skeletons range from a 90-foot-long diplodocus to a tiny *Thesalorsaurus neglectus* (so named because its bones sat neglected for years in a museum drawer before being reassembled).

On the same floor, the Hall of Mammals features 274 creatures, including lions and tigers and bears, plus more exotic animals from Australian tree kangaroos to a South American fairy armadillo. The star of the exhibit is a little, shrewlike creature, nicknamed "Morgie" for *Morganucodon oehleri*, one of the Earth's first mammals. Four-inch long Morgie foraged for food alongside the dinosaurs 210 million years ago. (A bronze sculpture depicts a slightly enlarged Morgie that is developing a shiny coat from being so frequently petted.) More interested in marine life? In the Sant Ocean Hall, a replica whale almost 50-feet long and a real-but-dead giant squid awe visitors.

MAKE THE MOST OF YOUR TIME
Drop into Discovery Center for hands-on activities or catch a film in the 487-seat Samuel C. Johnson IMAX Theater. For 3-D flicks, you get to don oversize glasses. No special specs are needed to see the Dinosaur Hall's triceratops. Scientists studied this massive herbivore (plant eater) by scanning bones and using computers to make a lifelike cast and video. Kids can compare it to what scientists in 1905 thought the triceratops looked like.

 Constitution Ave. and 10th St. NW.
Metro: Smithsonian

 Free

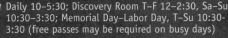 Daily 10–5:30; Discovery Room T–F 12–2:30, Sa–Su
10:30–3:30; Memorial Day–Labor Day, T–Su 10:30–
3:30 (free passes may be required on busy days)

 202/633–1000, 202/357–1729
TTY; www.mnh.si.edu

 2 and up, Discovery Room
4 and up

Other intriguing exhibits center on fossils, meteorites, and Egyptian mummies. Of course, the mammoth Hope Diamond is also here; the most-visited museum object in the world, it's even more popular than the *Mona Lisa*.

Not everything in the museum is dead or inanimate, though. To see animals in action, take your kids to the second floor's O. Orkin Insect Zoo, home to live ants, bees, centipedes, tarantulas, roaches, and other critters you wouldn't want in your house. After viewing these creepy creatures, young bug fanciers can act the part by crawling through a model of an African termite mound.

For a (literal) look at another fascinating species—the human being—kids can merge pictures of themselves with images of our ancestors in the Hall of Human Origins. This 15,000-square-foot exhibit explores how we evolved over 6 million years.

If you like this sight, you may also like the National Zoo (#25).

EATS FOR KIDS Tarantula feedings usually take place in the Insect Zoo at 10:30, 11:30, and 1:30 Tuesday through Friday and 11:30, 12:30, and 1:30 on weekends. Whereas the tarantulas' meal plan consists of the same old thing every day (crickets), you have lots of choices in the museum's 600-seat **Atrium Café** and the **Fossil Café**, where diners chow down at tables that have little fossilized artifacts and illustrations under glass.

KEEP IN MIND In the Insect Zoo roaches that freak out people are behind glass. But in the Butterfly Pavilion winged insects freely fly overhead.

NATIONAL MUSEUM OF THE U.S. NAVY

This museum is a "shore" thing for any child interested in naval gazing. Kids can spin the wheels of sailing ships, peer through periscopes, and turn and elevate 40-millimeter-long guns from World War II. All the while, they can get a maritime perspective on American history from the American Revolution to the present, including learning about the Navy's peacetime pursuits, such as diplomacy and humanitarian service. It is an especially good place to visit with a friend or relative who has served in the military.

Hands-on activities range from the no-tech (such as knot tying) to the high-tech (such as a Battle of Midway computer game in which children decipher coded messages). Free brochures listing activities for kids of all ages are available at the front desk. A kindergartner might do something as simple as draw a hat on a sailor or connect dots to make a plane; while older kids are encouraged to search for a silver sailor created from dimes or write slogans promoting military service.

MAKE THE MOST OF YOUR TIME

On weekends, there's plenty of parking on base. On weekdays, there is a paid parking lot for visitors across from the 6th and M Street gate.

EATS FOR KIDS

During the week, dine in or carry out food from the Navy Yard's **food court** and familiar harbors **Subway** and **Dunkin' Donuts.** On weekends, you have to bring your own meals. You can picnic any day alongside seagulls at waterside picnic tables in the shade or sun.

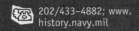 Washington Navy Yard, 11th and O Sts. SE.
Metro: Navy Yard (about 1 mile away)

 Free

 M–F 9–5; weekends and holidays 10–5; USS
Barry M–F 9–5, Sa and holidays 10–5

202/433-4882; www.
history.navy.mil

5 and up

If you call a few weeks in advance, you can arrange a special tour for your family or group. Themes might include Hats Off, during which kids learn about naval occupations by studying hats and then creating their own, or To the Ends of the Earth and Beyond, in which middle-schoolers study the Navy's role in polar and underwater explorations.

Outside the museum your family can board the decommissioned destroyer *Barry,* a vessel used during the Cuban Missile Crisis and the Vietnam War. Kids like the narrow halls, bunk beds, and mess hall, but they love taking the captain's wheel to "steer" the ship. Ahoy mates!

If you like this sight, you may also like the U.S. Navy Memorial across from the National Archives (#39).

KEEP IN MIND If your children say they want to become sailors, tell them about the "powder monkeys." During the War of 1812, Mexican War, and Civil War, sailors—always boys, as young as nine—carried gunpowder from the magazine to load the weapons. It was a dangerous job because these lads were often the targets of enemy fire. Learn more by playing games at asailorslifeforme.org.

NATIONAL MUSEUM OF
WOMEN IN THE ARTS

Every day is International Women's Day at this beautifully restored 1908 Renaissance Revival building, which spotlights works by prominent female artists from the Renaissance to the present day. Ironically, it was once a men-only Masonic temple. Now, in addition to traveling shows, the museum houses a permanent collection, including paintings, drawings, sculptures, prints, and photographs by such artists as Mary Cassatt, Frida Kahlo, Gabriele Münter, and Helen Frankenthaler.

As at many art museums, it can be difficult to pinpoint exactly what children will be drawn to. But they will likely appreciate the novelty of a sculpture that you can smell before you see it: Namely Chakaia Booker's *Acid Rain*, a piece made up of more than one ton of tires that she twisted, cut, and riveted. Nineteenth-century French artist Rosa Bonheur worked in a more traditional medium—paint—but her imaginative animal paintings, filled with rich and realistic textures, may also get kids talking. Teens, in particular, may enjoy contrasting their practical clothes (some, admittedly, more practical than others)

KEEP IN MIND It's hard for many kids to understand why it's important to have a museum devoted solely to women's works. To help them grasp the rationale, the staff may ask, "How many female artists can you name?" Here's another way to get your child interested in the art here: Ask about bugs. When Maria Sibylla Merian (born 1647) was about 14 years old, she started collecting, studying, and drawing insects. You can see her highly descriptive etchings and watercolors on display.

 1250 New York Ave. NW.
Metro: Metro Center

 202/783-5000 or 800/222-7270;
www.nmwa.org

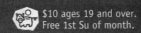 $10 ages 19 and over.
Free 1st Su of month.

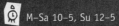 M–Sa 10–5, Su 12–5

 7 and up

with the ornate Renaissance-era clothing of the young woman in Lavinia Fontana's *Portrait of a Noblewoman* (1580).

Feeling inspired? Teaching artists lend their expertise to free family programs for children and teens several times per year. Topics reflect current exhibits, which could cover anything from photography to rock 'n roll. Reservations are required for most.

Whether you join a program or not you won't have to be here long to see that, though the artists showcased at the museum are limited to women, the approach to art and the appeal to visitors are universal.

If you like this sight, you might also like the Corcoran Gallery of Art (#62), the city's oldest art museum. You may find yourself trying to figure out which works are by women.

MAKE THE MOST OF YOUR TIME
At the information desk, pick up a pack of See for Yourself cards. These encourage close inspection of the art. Children too young to read can use the cards to play "I Spy," while parents can use the "something to talk about" prompts printed on each to discuss an artist's motivation or choice of materials with older children. Another conversation starter comes from the museum's website: Did you know only 5% of the art currently on display in U.S. museums is made by women?

EATS FOR KIDS
If white tablecloths aren't too formal, dine at the museum's **Mezzanine Café** (tel. 202/628-1068). For humbler fare and high chairs, try **Capitol City Brewing Company** (1100 New York Ave. NW, tel. 202/628-2222). **Haad Thai** (1100 New York Ave. NW, tel. 202/682-1111) serves crispy rolls and chicken skewers.

NATIONAL POSTAL MUSEUM

This museum gets a stamp of approval!

Look up and see one of the first airmail planes. Then look around and find first-class opportunities for children at this Smithsonian-operated museum dedicated to the history of our mail service and stamps. It's much smaller and less crowded than its cousins on the National Mall, so you can wander through in less than an hour.

Transportation-loving tots can pretend to move a lot of mail here. They can steer and push dozens of buttons on a full-size, big-rig truck cab right in the corner of the main exhibit area. Then they can experience what it was like to walk through the woods on route in the Binding the Nation exhibit by following a Native American trail that postal carriers once followed between New York and Boston. There aren't any signs to guide you. The only way to find the right route is to look for notches in the trees. Afterward, step up on a stagecoach and play postal worker in a railway car.

EATS FOR KIDS

Across the street, find something for even the pickiest eaters among the restaurants and 35-plus food stands in Union Station: **Johnny Rockets** (tel. 202/289–6969), a 1950s-style hamburger joint, is a family favorite. For other ideas, *see* listings under D.C. Ducks (#60).

MAKE THE MOST OF YOUR TIME Call or ask about activities
in the Discovery Center, near the statue of Ben Franklin, the first U.S. postmaster. Kids may play games, hear stories, and create crafts that reflect museum exhibits. Note that the museum is expected to grow in 2013 as a new street-level gallery devoted to stamps opens. So you may want to allow extra time for your visit.

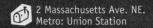 2 Massachusetts Ave. NE.
Metro: Union Station

 202/633-5535 or 202/633-1000, 202/633-9849 TTY; www.postalmuseum.si.edu

 Free

 Daily 10-5:30

 3 and up

In addition to all of the hands-on stuff here, the museum houses a cool collection of stamps. By pulling handles on vertical glass files, you can see foreign ones organized by country as well as U.S. ones organized by date, from 5- to 10-¢ stamps of 1847 to the latest issues. And if kids get curious about collecting stamps (a popular hobby 100 years ago), they can create their own online collections and email them home.

When you're ready to leave, consider purchasing a postcard from the museum's gift shop to send home by "snail mail."

If you like this sight, you may also like the National Geographic Museum (#35).

KEEP IN MIND While this museum helps give kids a new appreciation for their neighborhood postal workers, they might like to know that camels, birds, reindeer, and dogs have also helped deliver the mail. Although Owney the Dog never carried any, he was still the mascot of the railway mail service in the late 19th century. Thanks to taxidermy, you can actually see Owney at the museum.

NATIONAL ZOO

Known more for political animals than real animals, Washington nevertheless possesses one of the world's foremost zoos.

Start with any must-see creatures on your child's list. On busy days there may be waits at popular areas, such as the Giant Panda House, Reptile Discovery Center, Amazonia's tropical rain forest, or Elephant Trails. (Note: Kids like to peek at what's inside the thankfully plastic models of elephant poop at the Elephant Outpost.)

American Trail, which opened in September 2012, features North American mammals and birds, including seals and sea lions, wolves, beavers, and bald eagles. If your two-legged North American kids want to splash, they can do so in a little tide pool.

In the Bird House, flight is only restricted by the roof. Orangutans swing on overhead cables called the O-line from the Great Ape House to the Think Tank, where you can get a good look at the big apes while they get a better look at you.

Set among waterfalls, rocks, and bamboo grooves, the Asia Trail is home to red pandas, Asian small-clawed otters, sloth bears, clouded leopards, and the zoo's most popular

MAKE THE MOST OF YOUR TIME The Cleveland Park Metro stop is a better choice than Woodley Park/Zoo, with an uphill walk to the zoo but a downhill walk when you leave. Make sure your family wears comfortable shoes because the trek in is nothing compared to the walking you'll do over the zoo's 163 hilly acres. Rental strollers are available. Parking lots fill up in July and August, so arrive early. In summer, early morning (or late afternoon) is a better time to catch animals alert; in cooler months, they're more active at midday.

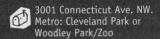
3001 Connecticut Ave. NW.
Metro: Cleveland Park or
Woodley Park/Zoo

 Free

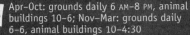
Apr–Oct: grounds daily 6 AM–8 PM, animal
buildings 10–6; Nov–Mar: grounds daily
6–6, animal buildings 10–4:30

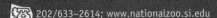 202/633–2614; www.nationalzoo.si.edu

 All ages

residents—the giant pandas. Adoring fans flock to these bears, which come from central China. The playful, high-profile giant pandas eat more than 50 pounds of bamboo every day.

To see the world's fastest feline, check out the Cheetah Conservation Area. To see animals with anywhere from zero to eight legs, visit the invertebrate exhibit, where octopuses, nautiluses, and giant spiders dwell.

If your child's idea of animals relates to lyrics with the letters E-I-E-I-O, try the Kids' Farm where you'll not only see animals that moo, neigh, cluck, and oink, you might get to help groom goats and miniature donkeys.

A trip to the zoo makes for an exhausting but fulfilling day. So pace yourselves; don't rush around trying to see everything. You can't. Watch your kids carefully; the biggest safety problem here is not animals but children wandering off.

If you like this sight, you may also like the National Aquarium (#40).

KEEP IN MIND
In D.C. stickers for FONZ (Friends of the National Zoo) are almost as ubiquitous as campaign bumper stickers. In addition to free parking and gift shop discounts, FONZ members can attend exclusive camps and classes or bed down at the zoo during members-only Snore & Roar sleepovers.

EATS FOR KIDS
The zoo's giant anteaters snack on peanut butter and the naked mole rats eat sweet potatoes and green beans. When hunger hits you, visit the **food kiosks** or restaurants like the **Mane Grill** (near the big cats) and the **Panda Overlook Cafe** (near—what else—the Giant Panda House), where you'll find grilled cheese sandwiches, pita sandwiches, and even animal cookies on the menu.

NEWSEUM

What is news and why is it, well, newsworthy? At this $450-million, 250,000-square-foot high-tech museum, you and your children can discover the story behind the headlines and even make some news of your own. Primarily funded by the Freedom Forum, a nonpartisan foundation dedicated to free press and free speech, the unique facility focuses on how and why news is made.

Fifteen theaters, another 15 galleries, two high-definition television studios, touch-screen timelines, and more tell the story of the news—not only of today but also of yesterday and tomorrow.

Because a lot of it concerns war and death, some exhibits in the Newseum may be perplexing or inappropriate for young children. You can't necessarily predict when you will come upon a graphic image, and screens constantly display up-to-date news items. So it's best to provide guidance throughout the visit if your children are under age 10 or particularly sensitive.

KEEP IN MIND

Extra! Extra! Read all about it! Don't let the ticket price put you off. Throughout the year (frequently on a three-day weekend), the museum hosts free or half-price days along with other deals.

MAKE THE MOST OF YOUR TIME

In less than 20 minutes, a 4-D movie in the Annenberg Theater covers three journalists in three centuries. Witness Isaiah Thomas reporting on the Battle of Lexington, Nellie Bly going undercover at a mental institution, and Edward R. Murrow broadcasting about the German blitz of London.

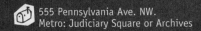
555 Pennsylvania Ave. NW.
Metro: Judiciary Square or Archives

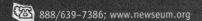
888/639-7386; www.newseum.org

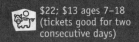
$22; $13 ages 7–18
(tickets good for two
consecutive days)

Daily 9–5

8 and up

With that said, intrepid young newshounds can easily occupy themselves. Through computers, your kids can experience what it's like to be a reporter or editor. They'll contemplate the ethics of anonymous sources and bias. Some questions may transfer to the lives of preteens and teens. For example as a reporter, you find out that your neighbor has been arrested. Do you tell your editor?

Or your kids might like to go on camera, reading the news from a real monitor as a video backdrop (choices include the White House and the National Zoo) appears behind them. Later you can download it from the Newseum website!

Journalists are known for asking poignant questions. After visiting this museum of news, your child should have a lot to talk about.

If you like this sight, you might also like the International Spy Museum (#51).

EATS FOR KIDS For a bite without leaving the building, try the **Food Section** on the concourse level. The cafeteria seats 152. If you'd rather treat your future Katie Couric or Jon Stewart to a more formal meal at the museum, consider the **Source by Wolfgang Puck** (tel. 202/637–6100). On the street level, the Source is a grill but upstairs it's fine dining.

OXON COVE PARK

If you want to rewind to a time when taking care of the animals meant more than walking the family dog or feeding the cat, visit this working farm (also called Oxon Hill Farm) administered by the National Park Service. Established on a site where the Piscataway Indians once lived, it has animals and equipment typical of life in a bygone era—mostly the early 19th century and later.

Down on this farm you can find draft horses, sheep, pigs, ducks, geese, turkeys, cows, and goats (known as poor man's cows because they're capable of eating just about anything and still producing milk and cheese). Many children's favorite animal is the milk cow that doesn't have horns. Unlike their 19th-century counterparts, most modern farmers stunt the growth of horns, as they're a hazard to farmers and other cows and no longer needed for protection.

With supervision, your children can milk a cow, collect eggs warm from the nest, and toss corn to feed the chickens. Hayrides depart at 1:30 PM, except on Friday, when they leave at 11 AM.

EATS FOR KIDS For fresh food, bring your own and take advantage of picnic tables set out in the shade near the parking lot, along the path to the farm, or near the house. A vending machine is stocked with water and juices but no sodas. Otherwise, your options consist of National Harbor (*see #34*), where you have to pay to park, or **fast-food outlets** and an **Outback Steakhouse** (6091 Oxon Hill Rd., tel. 301/839–4300) a few miles away on Oxon Hill Road.

6411 Oxon Hill Rd., Oxon Hill, MD

 Free

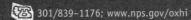 301/839-1176; www.nps.gov/oxhi

 Daily 8–4:30

 1–11

A furnished parlor in a white farmhouse owned by the DeButts family in the early 1800s is open a few times each week. Park rangers and volunteers are usually on hand to talk about the British-born Mrs. DeButts and her views on slavery and the War of 1812. Call ahead to find out when kids can participate in daily chores and when the farmhouse is open.

Oxon Cove Park offers free, farm-fresh programs, including sheep shearing in May, cider making in September, corn harvesting in October, and "Talking Turkey" in November. Junior ranger programs in the summertime teach 9- to 12-year-olds about farm life. Reservations for all programs are a must.

If you like this sight, you may also like the Kids' Farm at the National Zoo (#25).

KEEP IN MIND

People often think pigs are dumb, yet some farmers believe they learn more quickly than horses and dogs. One popular conception that does hold true concerns their trough manners. Watch as the cows' milk is delivered to them. Then ask your kids if they like pigs!

MAKE THE MOST OF YOUR TIME The farm gets the most visitors during spring and fall when school groups come, but there's always parking and plenty of room for everyone to explore. Whenever you visit, remind your children to move slowly near the animals and not to make any loud noises or sudden motions as such actions are likely to startle the critters. Though you will no doubt get a kick out of watching your child get a (figurative) kick out of the animals, also take a moment to appreciate the panoramic view of Washington over the Potomac River.

PATUXENT NATIONAL WILDLIFE
VISITOR CENTER

What kind of noise does a bluejay make? How does a katydid sound? What about a beaver? Your kids are bound to find out here. The first stop at the Patuxent Research Refuge is the Nature Calls kiosk: no spelling, reading, or typing is required to learn about the refuge's animals at this animated game in the lobby. But that's just the beginning as kids track down animals inside and outside this huge modern nature center.

Older kids might want to hang around Nature Calls to set up a rap session for birds, while younger kids may prefer to skip ahead to view Handles on Habitat, where they can pull a knob to see a pelican and osprey appear in the Chesapeake Bay or push a button to watch a scientist pop up with a mirror to look at birds' nests in the Hawaiian rainforest. Life-size dioramas of wild animals depict whooping cranes, timber wolves, and California sea otters swimming in kelp. The exhibits have enough buttons and knobs to amuse even toddlers.

MAKE THE MOST OF YOUR TIME

A 35-minute narrated tram tour runs through the refuge's meadows, forests, and wetlands, weather permitting. Though the narrator's commentary about wildlife management may be too advanced for your children, they'll probably find the ride itself sufficiently thrilling.

Patuxent hosts hunts, hikes, and activities for naturalists of all ages throughout the year. For example, preschoolers are advised to "dress to get dirty" for Whacky Wetlands,

EATS FOR KIDS Picnicking is not allowed, but on a pleasant day you can bring snacks to eat on the visitor center patio. Otherwise, the staff at the front desk can direct you to local **fast-food eateries**, many of which are along Route 197. A 15-minute drive away in Laurel, **Pasta Plus** (209 Gorman Ave., tel. 301/498–5100) serves up homemade pastas, breads, and desserts, which you can also carry out.

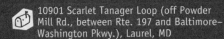

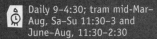
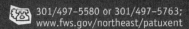

while Dragonflies of Patuxent teaches kids 12 and up how to identify these ferocious predators of the pond. The Kids Fishing Day held in early June attracts hundreds of anglers hoping for the big one.

You can take your own wildlife tour by following the well-marked trails. The paved Wildlife Loop is wide enough for a double stroller but short enough (about ⅓ mile) so that preschoolers won't wear out. At the bird-viewing blind, even the youngest members of the family (with a boost from you) can peer through a slat as birds swoop within a few inches of their faces. Another 4 miles of trails, made of wood chips and other natural materials, satisfy junior and senior naturalists.

If you like this sight, you may also like Rock Creek Park (#19).

KEEP IN MIND You may be tempted to leave most of your cash at home because, with the exception of the tram ride, all activities are free. However, do bring a little money for the Wildlife Images Bookstore, which sells some interesting children's merchandise at reasonable prices. Your offspring might like stickers, rubber creatures, posters, or playing cards with pictures of endangered animals on them. Profits benefit the refuge.

PHILLIPS COLLECTION

This kid-comfortable museum, where you can sit back on a puffy couch or plop down on the carpet, was formerly the home—albeit the grand one—of founder Duncan Phillips. In his onetime residence and in similarly scaled additions that retain the intimacy of a private abode, you'll see works by impressionists, plus modern and contemporary American and European artists. Six fireplaces (and a fake one which looks real) add to the museum's homey feel. Unlike most other galleries, where uniformed guards appear uninterested in the masterpieces around them, the Phillips employs art students to sit by the paintings and answer questions.

The collection's best-known piece, Pierre-Auguste Renoir's *Luncheon of the Boating Party*, is particularly interesting to children because its colors are bright, the people in it are engaged in happy conversation, and there's a terrier on the table. Kids can also relate to subjects like a ballet rehearsal, by Edgar Degas; a bullfight, by Pablo Picasso; and a game of hide-and-seek, by William Merritt Chase. Works by Swiss artist Paul Klee also appeal to

MAKE THE MOST OF YOUR TIME The Gallery and eight other "off the Mall" museums in the greater Dupont Circle area open their doors for free during the first weekend in June. Find the full list of museums and details at www.dkmuseums.com.

1600 21st St. NW.
Metro: Dupont Circle

202/387-2151;
www.phillipscollection.org

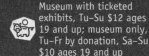
Museum with ticketed exhibits, Tu–Su $12 ages 19 and up; museum only, Tu–Fr by donation, Sa–Su $10 ages 19 and up

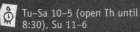
Tu–Sa 10–5 (open Th until 8:30), Su 11–6

5 and up

kids. His small-scale paintings include many kinds of symbols—even some which look like hieroglyphs. But perhaps the artwork that will have the greatest impact is on the bottom floor of the museum's Sant building where contributions by local students are proudly displayed as part of the Young Artists Exhibition Program.

Gather a group of five or more kids and call four weeks in advance for a personal tour that includes interactive activities led by the museum's enthusiastic education staff. If you don't have time to book ahead or if the idea of being with more than a couple of kids seems daunting, you can download a Discovery Pack (and impress your kids with your knowledge) or pick one up at the museum entrance. Each pack includes artwork to examine, postcards or pictures, and activities you can try at home so the fun continues long after you've left.

If you like this sight, you may also like the National Gallery of Art (#36).

KEEP IN MIND The Phillips Collection staff requests that everyone turn off their cell phones in the gallery. Also, keep a safe distance—24 inches—from all paintings and sculpture, because artwork can be damaged by accident.

EATS FOR KIDS You can buy sandwiches, salads, and pastries at the **Tryst of the Phillips** (tel. 202/387-2151 Ext. 351) in the gallery overlooking a courtyard. Open 10–4 Tuesday through Saturday and 11–5 on Sunday, it has high chairs but no booster seats. A better bet for a quick bite may be one of the many inexpensive spots around Dupont Circle. For pizza, gyros, and Greek concoctions, try **Zorba's Café** (1612 20th St. NW, tel. 202/387-8555). At **Kramer Books and Afterwards Café** (1517 Connecticut Ave. NW, tel. 202/387-3825), you can buy a book and enjoy it with breakfast, lunch, or dinner.

PRESIDENT LINCOLN'S COTTAGE

Washington is full of A+ places for young Honest Abe scholars. But this spot offers a unique perspective on a legendary leader who came from humble beginnings.

If your children are expecting to see an old house full of fancy furnishings, they'll be disappointed. The rooms are almost barren. Nevertheless, guides who are master storytellers bring them to life with tales of what it was like for Lincoln and his family to live here when the president wasn't at the White House.

In June 1862, President Lincoln—together with his wife Mary, and nine-year-old son Tad—moved from the White House to this Gothic Revival cottage on the grounds of the Soldiers' Home to escape the oppressive heat of Washington and to mourn the loss of his 11-year-old son Willie. Lincoln lived in the cottage from June to November 1862, 1863, and 1864—that's a quarter of his presidency.

MAKE THE MOST OF YOUR TIME

About four times a year, the Cottage hosts free special events that may include Civil War encampments with reenactments, live music, munchies, a petting zoo, and people in period costumes. Sometimes kids even get to top off their day with—what else?—a top hat!

EATS FOR KIDS The on-site **gift shop** sells old-fashioned candies, like peanut brittle and candied rose petals, plus a few modern treats, such as granola bars. You're welcome to picnic on the grounds where soldiers have eaten for centuries. Consider snacks that Lincoln liked: biscuits, nuts, cheese and crackers, and fresh fruits, especially apples. Looking for something more substantial? Fried chicken, collard greens, and mac-and-cheese make the menu at the nearby **Hitching Post** (200 Upshur St., NW, tel. 202/726–1511) work for many kids.

 Rock Creek Church Rd. and Upshur St. NW. (approx. 140 Rock Creek Church Rd., NW for GPS)

 202/829-0436; www.lincolncottage.org

 $15 ages 13 and up, $5 aged 6–12

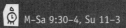 M-Sa 9:30-4, Su 11-3

 6 and up

Tours run every hour from 10 to 3, Monday through Saturday, and every hour from noon to 4 on Sunday. Only 20 spots are available per tour, so advance reservations through the website are recommended.

One-hour tours start with a short film followed by a stop in front of a life-size statue of Lincoln and his horse. (Hint: Great photo op.) Inside the home, guides tell stories and explain the sights and sounds Lincoln would have heard while drafting the Emancipation Proclamation here. Younger children might prefer hearing about how he tucked notes into his top hat or about the time he was woken up in the middle of the night to greet a distinguished visitor from London. Surprisingly, Lincoln met the guest in his pajamas and spent most of the evening talking about his own childhood.

If you like this sight, you might like to tip your hat to Lincoln—and see the top hat he himself tipped—at the National Museum of American History (#32).

KEEP IN MIND. In the 1860s, Lincoln could get here on horseback from the White House in 30 minutes. Today you can drive it in about half that time, provided it's not rush hour and there's no presidential motorcade. If you come by cab, the Cottage's website advises you to tell the driver you're going to the Armed Forces Retirement Home or "Old Soldiers' Home. (The website also has how-to tips for renting bikes or reserving a car service.) If you opt to take metro, follow the green/yellow line to the Georgia Ave.–Petworth stop; then catch the H8 bus to the cottage.

ROCK CREEK PARK

On the biggest stretch of parkland in Washington you can truly take a walk on the wild side. Begin at the nature center, which brings the outdoors in. Upstairs, pelts, bones, feathers, and a bird's nest occupy a touch table near stuffed animals that are representative of park residents. Preschoolers put on puppet shows featuring their forest friends in the Discovery Room. Downstairs, elementary schoolchildren use mice (the computer kind) to learn more about the park's ecosystem. A 75-seat planetarium introduces youngsters to the solar system, and some shows include a Native American legend about a coyote that threw rocks to make pictures in the sky.

You can take a hike on any of several trails near the center. The 15- to 20-minute Edge of the Woods trail—a flat, asphalt loop perfect for preschoolers and strollers—goes to a pond a little larger than a bathtub. For older children, the Woodland Trail takes 40–60 minutes. On most weekends, rangers lead hikes themed around topics ranging from the lowly worm to the majestic wolf.

EATS FOR KIDS To wet your whistle, you can take a sip from the water fountain or purchase a bottle of water at the center. For anything else, you're on your own. Picnic areas are nearby, so one option is to pack a lunch from **Magruder's Grocery Store** (5626 Connecticut Ave. NW, tel. 202/244–7800), a 5- to 10-minute drive from the nature center. Near Magruder's are two inexpensive restaurants: **American City Diner** (5532 Connecticut Ave. NW, tel. 202/244–1949) and, for those who like éclairs, cookies, and other sweet treats, **Bread and Chocolate** (5542 Connecticut Ave. NW, tel. 202/966–7413).

5200 Glover Rd. NW; stables 5100 Glover Rd. NW (between 16th St. and Connecticut Ave., south of Military Rd.)

 202/895-6070 nature center, 202/362-0117 stables; www.nps.gov/rocr or www.rockcreekhorsecenter.com

 Free; pony rides $20 for 15 min; trail rides $40 per hr

 Daily sunrise–sunset; nature center W–Su 9–5; pony rides Apr–Oct T, W, Th 3 and 3:30, Sa–Su 1–3:30; trail rides T, W, and Th 6 pm, Sa 9:30–12:30, Su 11–2

 2 and up, pony rides 4–7, trail rides 12 and up

If your boots aren't made for walking, why not saddle up? Rock Creek is the only place inside the city where kids can become urban cowboys and cowgirls (closed-toe shoes, preferably with a small heel, are mandatory). Pony rides (reservations required) aren't just a trip around a circle, but rather 15-minute rides through the woods. They'll take children as young as 2½ and as old as 11. Many preschoolers, though, aren't ready for this excursion, and kids over eight might find it babyish. On one-hour trail rides, guides take groups along some of the same wooded trails that presidents Martin Van Buren, Teddy Roosevelt, and Ronald Reagan once rode.

If you like this sight, you might also like the United States National Arboretum (#8).

KEEP IN MIND

Youngsters 6 to 12 can ask for a Junior Ranger activity book. After completing at least six of the dozen activities, staff will reward their hard work with either a Junior Ranger patch or a badge that looks like the ones worn by park rangers.

MAKE THE MOST OF YOUR TIME The planetarium offers free weekend shows at 1 for ages five and up (also on Wednesday at 4 for ages four and up) and at 4 for ages seven and up. Children four and under may find these either boring or scary. (Before shows, the sun is shown setting over the Washington skyline; at the end, it rises and the room brightens.) Afterward, the rangers will give you a sheet showing the stars that you can see in the sky this month.

ROOSEVELT ISLAND

18

If the wildest animal your children ever want to see is an angry bird, Roosevelt Island isn't for your family. But for kids who believe, as Theodore Roosevelt did, that "There is delight in the hardy life of the open," this sanctuary is a superb place to get away from the city's concrete, crowds, and cars. If it weren't for the airplanes from Ronald Reagan National Airport roaring overhead, you might forget you were in D.C. altogether.

The Island is a little tricky to reach as you'll need to be driving west on the George Washington Memorial Parkway. Leave your car in the lot next to the George Washington Memorial Parkway and walk over the bridge to this island wilderness preserve in the Potomac River. The 88.5-acre tribute to the conservation-minded 26th president includes 2½ miles of nature trails that crisscross marshland, swampland, and upland forest.

In the center of the island is a clearing where a 17-foot bronze statue of Roosevelt stands, his right hand raised for emphasis. He is surrounded by shallow pools, fountains, and

KEEP IN MIND

How did the Rough Rider known for carrying "a big stick" inspire a stuffed animal? Once, when Roosevelt was hunting, aides tied up an old bear for him to kill. But he couldn't shoot the defenseless animal, prompting a toymaker to create the teddy bear.

MAKE THE MOST OF YOUR TIME After crossing the bridge you'll see a large bulletin board where you can pick up a brochure with a map. Encourage children to stay on marked trails. Off them you may encounter poison ivy and great nettles. The latter (which can grow as tall as 3 feet) is better known as stinging nettles because you can feel a stinging pain if you rub against it. Gather a group of 10 or more people and call two weeks in advance to request a ranger-led tour. Your guide will point out much more than where the stinging nettles are.

four large stone tablets inscribed with his thoughts on nature, manhood, state (government), and youth. For example, Roosevelt advised students at the Groton School in Massachusetts, "Keep your eyes on the stars, but remember to keep your feet on the ground." And there is plenty of ground for your feet to cover here.

To make the most of your visit, load up a backpack with some of the following items for your children: binoculars, a magnifying glass, a sketch pad and crayons or markers, a camera, and plant and animal guidebooks, if you have them. Cattails, arrow arum, pickerelweed, willow, ash, maple, and oak all grow on the island, which is also a habitat for frogs, raccoons, birds, squirrels, deer, and the occasional red or gray fox. But you won't see the animal most people associate with Roosevelt: the teddy bear.

If you like this sight, you may also like to see a memorial built in honor of Teddy's cousin Franklin (#57).

EATS FOR KIDS There's nothing to buy on this island—not even a soda. (Of course, you may not want to drink too much anyway because public restrooms close between late October and early April.) The Park Service requests that you don't eat too close to the memorial, and there aren't any tables here. So you'll want to bring your own blanket if you plan to picnic. Listen to the music of birds and the planes overhead as you eat.

Imagine your child making a gold mirror or drawing animes while learning about ancient art techniques, geography, and other cultures. It's all part of the innovative ImaginAsia program. Armed with guidebook and pencil, children (and their parents) may search for heroes and monsters, lotus flowers, wild horses in ceramics, sculptures, and paintings or go on a journey along the legendary Silk Road. The program is operated on a drop-in basis, but it's usually best to arrive on time, as seats fill fast; reservations are only required for groups of eight or more.

Even if you're not visiting on a program day, there's a lot here to interest your kids. Activity-filled guidebooks are available at each museum's information desk. And just why, you might be wondering, are there two Asian museums? The Freer Gallery, which contains one of the world's finest collections of Asian masterpieces, was endowed by Charles Freer, who insisted on a few conditions: Objects in the collection could not be loaned out, nor could objects from outside the collection be put on display. Because of the latter, the

KEEP IN MIND While you're in the Peacock Room, think about the real peacocks that used to live at the gallery. In 1993 a peacock named James and a peahen named Sylvia resided in the museum's courtyard. After one year, the gallery needed to find a new home for the birds because Sylvia laid too many eggs. The pair moved in with a farmer who loved them because they squawked to alert her when visitors arrived.

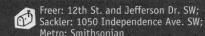 Freer: 12th St. and Jefferson Dr. SW;
Sackler: 1050 Independence Ave. SW;
Metro: Smithsonian

 Free

 Daily 10–5:30

 202/633–4880 or 202/633–1000,
202/633–5285 TTY; www.asia.si.edu

 7 and up

connected Sackler Gallery was built. Like the Freer, the Sackler focuses on works from throughout Asia, but it mounts visiting exhibits as well.

The Freer's collection also includes works by American artists influenced by Asia. One such was Freer's friend James McNeill Whistler, who encouraged him to collect Asian art. On display in Gallery 12 is Whistler's Peacock Room, a blue-and-gold Victorian dining room, complete with painted leather, gilded wood shelving, and a canvas ceiling that is, as the name implies, decorated with peacocks. Freer moved the entire room from London to the United States in 1904.

If you like this sight, you may also like the National Museum of African Art (#33).

EATS FOR KIDS

For restaurant choices, *see* listings under any of the museums on the Mall: the Castle, Museum of the American Indian, National Air and Space Museum, National Gallery of Art and Sculpture Garden, National Museum of American History, and National Museum of Natural History.

MAKE THE MOST OF YOUR TIME Plan on an Ima-
ginAsia program most weekends at 2 or on summer afternoons. Although geared toward children between the ages of 8 and 14, teachers often welcome younger children on less crowded days. If yours love the experience, consider signing them up for a weeklong summer residency program. These are aimed at young artists ages 9 to 18.

SIX FLAGS AMERICA

Washington is known for its educational and economical attractions. Six Flags America, the capital area's only theme park, isn't either—but it is exciting. Actually a combination theme park and water park (dubbed Hurricane Harbor), the facility contains more than 100 rides, shows, and games spread over 150 acres in suburban Prince George's County.

On the "dry" side, roller-coaster revelers have eight fast choices. The Wild One (dating back to 1917) is a classic wooden coaster. Roar mixes old-fashioned wood and modern computer technology to produce a thrilling ride. The five steel coasters are Batwing, Superman-Ride of Steel, the Mind Eraser, the Joker's Jinx, and the Apocalypse. Coaster traditionalists prefer the jiggle and clackety-clack sounds of the "woodie." Metal versions follow a more circuitous route, with corkscrew turns and 360-degree loops. If your youngsters aren't tall enough (all rides, including the coasters, have height restrictions), head to Thomas Town, which is named after the famous tank engine and designed for the six and under set.

MAKE THE MOST OF YOUR TIME

Lines form on weekends before the park even opens. To avoid crowds, come on Monday or Tuesday (ideally with a route planned out), and do what most interests your kids first.

EATS FOR KIDS Approximately 10,000 pounds of sugar are used to make the roughly 100,000 servings of candy sold here annually—the same amount you'd use if you felt like baking nearly 1½ million chocolate-chip cookies. As in other theme parks, food is expensive. You can pack a picnic but must eat it outside of the park because no food can be brought in. One sealed bottle of water per person is permitted. (Vendors also provide complimentary cups of water and ice inside.) On-site there are loads of eateries. **Johnny Rockets, Heritage House,** and (for season pass holders only) **Crazy Horse Saloon** are air-conditioned.

13710 Central Ave. (Rte. 214), Bowie/Mitchellville, MD

301/249-1500; www.sixflags.com/america

$60 48" and over, $38 children 3 and up under 48" (add 10% entertainment tax); parking $17

Mid-Apr-May, Sa–Su 10:30–6; Memorial Day–mid-June, M–F 10:30–6, Sa–Su 10:30–9; mid-June–mid-Aug, daily 10:30–7, Sa–Su 10:30–9 2nd wk in Aug 10:30–6, last wk of Aug open weekend only. Labor Day weekend Sa–Su 10:30–9, M 10:30–8; Oct weekends only

2 and up

On the "wet" side, kids like Crocodile Cal's Caribbean Beach House. Water-powered activities here include a barrel that dumps 1,000 gallons of water on unsuspecting passersby every few minutes. The Hurricane Bay wave pool has a graduated entrance so even water babies (with parents, of course) can splash around, but an even better bet for little ones might be Buccaneer Beach. In a twist on standard height restrictions, anyone over 54-inches tall must accompany a kid. Just be aware that if you're spending time at Hurricane Harbor Water Park, you'll have to plan on getting out of your soaking swimsuits a bit early. Six Flag's "wet" component closes one hour before the "dry" park does.

If you like this sight, you may also like National Harbor (#34), another attraction in Prince George's County, MD.

KEEP IN MIND To maximize your chances of minimizing expenses and aggravation, plan ahead. By ordering tickets online three days in advance, you can save a bundle. Also, local grocery stores and fast-food restaurants often have coupons. To find who is currently offering them, call Six Flags and ask to speak with a representative from guest services. Season pass holders also receive discounts at other Six Flags parks. If your child needs a stroller, bring your own to save the rental fee.

Visiting here provides a one-two punch because the American Art Museum and the National Portrait Gallery—both part of the Smithsonian Institution—share space in the same grand old building.

Pieces in the Smithsonian American Art Museum emphasize technique and aesthetic appeal as opposed to subject matter. This museum is home to one of the largest collections of American art in the world: a collection that spans more than three centuries and contains lots folk art and fine crafts that kids can relate to. At the National Portrait Gallery, on the other hand, the emphasis is on the subject. From presidents to sports heroes to military figures, they're here in some form, including photographs, paintings, sculptures, and drawings.

Even if the distinction between the two types of art is lost on kids, most will find James Hampton's work interesting. Ask your son what he would do with an empty garage. Ask your daughter what she would do with hundreds of rolls of aluminum foil. Check out what

EATS FOR KIDS You can pick up a premade sandwich at nearby **Cowgirl Creamery** (919 F St. NW, tel. 202/393–6880). The self-titled cheese shop has an educated staff that can help you find the perfect cheese while offering your kids a variety of stickers. Otherwise, purchase American fare at the museums' own **Courtyard café** (202/633–5465). Even if you're not hungry, the expansive, light-filled Kogod Courtyard is a great place to unwind.

8th and F Sts. NW.
Metro: Gallery Place-Chinatown Metrorail station

 Free

Daily 11:30–7

202/633-7970; americanart.si.edu Art Museum
202/633-8300; www.npg.si.edu Portrait Gallery

4 and up

Hampton did when he was working as a janitor. For more than 12 years he built a huge throne using salvaged objects and what amounts to reams of silver and gold foils. His shiny *Throne of the Third Heaven of the Nations Millennium General Assembly*, referred to as the *Hampton Throne*, captivates kids of all ages. An unknown artist created *Bottlecap Giraffe* in the late 1960s. (No word on whether he or she drank all the sodas to get the caps.) Another artist, Nam June Paik, created a piece called *Electronic Superhighway: Continental U.S., Alaska, Hawaii*, using 343 televisions.

The Portrait Gallery has the only complete collection of presidential portraits outside of the White House. Ask your kids to find the sculpture of the president playing horseshoes.

If you like this sight, you may also like the Sculpture Garden at the National Gallery of Art (#36).

MAKE THE MOST OF YOUR TIME

These museums share the Lunder Conservation Center on the third floor, where conservators examine, treat, and preserve artwork. If they're not busy doing any of the above when you arrive, you can watch a 40-foot media wall that shows them at work.

KEEP IN MIND At the front desk, ask for a Portrait Discovery kit, which includes everything kids need to create their own self-portrait, write a label, and even compare it with a portrait of a doll. The Smithsonian American Art Museum offers free art programs one Saturday a month. Activities might include chalk drawing on the sidewalk, making baseball cards, and painting on canvas. Scavenger hunts are available every day in the museum's Luce Foundation Center.

SULLY HISTORIC SITE

This place gives kids a real feel for life in the Federal Period (1790–1820). Some may pretend to wash dishes in an old stone sink or cool off with a folded fan. Others may take a whiff of No. 7, a cologne that George Washington (and more recently John F. Kennedy) wore. But kids will also learn that life wasn't so sweet then, and not just because the early 1800s lacked our modern amenities. Slavery is addressed, and your children can handle replicas of the passes that slaves needed to leave the property, or lift the heavy cast ironware they used in the kitchen.

Before becoming a living history museum, Sully (built in 1794) was the understated country home of Richard Bland Lee, uncle of Confederate general Robert E. Lee; his wife, Elizabeth Collins Lee; and their children. As Virginia's first representative to Congress, Lee cast one of two swing votes that put the nation's capital in his backyard.

Guides, often Fairfax County Park Authority volunteers, conduct one-hour tours of the Lee house on the hour. If the guides don't point it out, challenge your child to find

KEEP IN MIND

Some of the stairs in the Sully mansion are steep, so make sure unsteady toddlers, unsteady grandparents, and distracted parents are extra careful. Strollers are not permitted in the house, but the first floor is wheelchair accessible.

MAKE THE MOST OF YOUR TIME
At least one weekend each month, Sully hosts special events. For example, it stages a car show on Father's Day and celebrates Colonial Day on the first weekend in November. Admission may be up to $4 extra during these times but there's more to do and see.

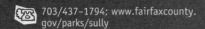

the white squirrel in the parlor. When the Lee children were living here, their pet white squirrel was let loose in the house! On request, the guides may tailor their talk to your family's special interests (textiles or cooking, for example).

Your children might also enjoy seeing the one-room log schoolhouse that was used in nearby Haymarket during the early to mid-19th century. In this tiny room, where visitors now purchase tickets and souvenirs, about a half-dozen children probably studied under a teacher who lived above the classroom.

Weather permitting, there is also a Forgotten Road Tour of the outbuildings, including reconstructed slave dwellings, at 2 (early March–mid-November). Most spring and summer weekends are especially festive, with such special activities as quill pen writing, biscuit baking, and children's games.

If you like this sight, you may also like another grand old home, the Frederick Douglass National Historic Site (#56).

EATS FOR KIDS Inside the site's little schoolhouse you can purchase candy sticks (a treat that kids have enjoyed since the 1800s) along with assorted other vintage sweets. In summer, ice cream is also available. For meals, there are many options to choose from on Route 50, including **Cici's Pizza** (14392 Chantilly Crossing La., tel. 703/961–9100), an all-you-can-eat place, and **Five Guys Burgers and Fries** (14421 Chantilly Crossing La., tel. 703/817–7718), which sells two things—burgers and hot dogs.

THOMAS JEFFERSON MEMORIAL

Many children and adults may be surprised to learn that Thomas Jefferson didn't list being the third president as one of his greatest accomplishments. When he appraised his own life, Jefferson wanted to be remembered as the "Author of the Declaration of American Independence, of the Statute of Virginia for religious freedom, and Father of the University of Virginia."

The memorial honoring him is the southernmost of the District's major monuments and memorials, four long blocks and a trip around the Tidal Basin from the Metro. Jefferson had always admired the Pantheon in Rome (the rotundas he designed for the University of Virginia and his own Monticello were inspired by its dome), so architect John Russell Pope drew from the same source when he designed this memorial. Even children who have never heard of Rome, not to mention Jefferson, will appreciate the view of the White House (one of the city's best) afforded by the memorial's top steps.

KEEP IN MIND Every spring, Washington eagerly waits for the delicate flowers of the cherry trees (many of which are near the memorial) to bloom. Park-service experts try their best to predict when the buds will pop—usually for about 10–12 days at the beginning of April. But regardless of when they flower, the two-week long National Cherry Blossom Festival (*see* www.nationalcherryblossomfestival.org for dates and information) is celebrated with the lighting of a ceremonial Japanese lantern, fashion shows, and a parade. When the weather complies and the blossoms are at their peak for the festival, Washington rejoices.

 Tidal Basin South Bank off Ohio Dr. SW.
Metro: Smithsonian

 24 hrs; staffed daily 9:30 AM–11:30 PM

 Free

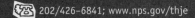 202/426-6841; www.nps.gov/thje

5 and up

Inside, a 19-foot bronze statue of Jefferson on a 6-foot granite pedestal looms larger than life. And just in case your children didn't take the National Park Service ranger recommendation to research Jefferson before visiting the memorial, they can learn about this Renaissance man by reading his writings about freedom and government on marble walls surrounding the statue. The whole family can take advantage of ranger-led programs offered throughout the day or ask questions of the ranger on duty.

An exhibit called Light and Liberty, on the lower level, provides highlights of Jefferson's life together with a timeline of world history during his era, and a 10-minute video. When you've seen it all, you and your children can judge for yourselves what Jefferson's greatest accomplishments really were.

If you like this sight, you may also like the Lincoln Memorial (#48).

MAKE THE MOST OF YOUR TIME

Allow about five hours to tour the monuments in Washington. Mid-April through November, you might want to set aside an additional hour for a paddleboat ride in the Tidal Basin (1501 Maine Ave. SW, tel. 202/479-2426; www.tidalbasinpeddleboats.com). You can see the dock from the Memorial.

EATS FOR KIDS Rumor has it that some critics called the memorial "Jefferson's muffin" based on its shape. A short drive away in East Potomac Park is **Potomac Grille** (972 Ohio Dr. SW, at Maine Ave., tel. 202/554-7660), where you can get blueberry muffins (along with jumbo burgers and sandwiches) at more reasonable prices than most Mall vendors. There's also a minigolf course there.

TYSONS CORNER CENTER'S
AMERICAN GIRL STORE

Brace yourself. This pink-and-white shop is just as much a testament to marketing as it is to the popularity of *American Girl* books and dolls.

Located in Tysons Corner Center (tel. 703/847–7300; www.shoptysons.com), one of the largest malls in the country, the American Girl store not only sells dolls and related accessories ranging from sports equipment to pets, it's also a place for pampering in the doll salon and dining with dolls in an on-site bistro.

For the uninitiated, American Girl dolls portray 9- to 11–year-old girls who "star" in books told from the girls' own viewpoint. Originally the stories focused on different periods of American history, but contemporary tales were added in 1995. Owned by Mattel, the dolls include traditional American Girl dolls and "My" American Girl dolls (which are the same size and shape but different in coloring and hair styles), along with Bitty Baby and Bitty Twins dolls for younger children.

KEEP IN MIND

Boys could be extremely bored here. Let them get their own toy fix in the hands-on play section of the LEGO Store (tel. 703/848–2822) on the first level of Tysons Corner Center. It's right around the corner from the American Girl store.

MAKE THE MOST OF YOUR TIME

The website refers to this location as Washington, D.C. But it's actually in the Northern Virginia suburbs, about 12 miles from the center of the city, and not yet accessible by Metro. The local "rush hour" (which tends to be the opposite of rush and lasts several hours), doesn't keep families from driving long distances for the American Girl experience. Travelers can arrange to have special beds for the dolls at hotels in both Northern Virginia and Washington, D.C. The store's website lists options.

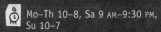

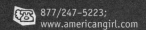

1961 Chain Bridge Rd., Tysons Corner, VA

877/247–5223;
www.americangirl.com

Window shopping
free; merchandise and
services vary

Mo–Th 10–8, Sa 9 AM–9:30 PM,
Su 10–7

3–12

In the salon, dolls can get their hair styled and their ears pierced. Girls hoping to do the same will have to go elsewhere. Salon services are just for dolls.

But everyone can dine at the 110-seat bistro for lunch, dinner, or tea. The menu contains perennial kid-pleasers like chicken noodle soup and macaroni with "lots of cheese" as well as fancier fare, including fresh fruit with yogurt sauce and roasted salmon with mushroom orzo. Top it off with an ice-cream sundae or a lollipop brownie. Tea includes mini muffins, sandwiches, and pink cupcakes. A less expensive option is ordering a dessert at the counter, which looks like an old-fashioned soda fountain.

Looking for a no-cost alternative? Girls get creative here with art activities several times a week. You don't need to make reservations for free activities, which tend to be quick crafts made from paper, such as cards, bonnets, and—you guessed it—paper dolls!

If you like this sight, your daughter may also enjoy bringing her doll to the old-fashion home at the Sully Historic Site (#14)

EATS FOR KIDS If you'd rather eat elsewhere or you don't have time to wait, Tysons Corner Center has 47 other food choices, including **BGR The Burger Joint** (tel. 703/790–3437), **California Pizza Kitchen** (tel. 703/761–1473), and the fancier **Seasons 52** (tel. 703/288–3852), which serves mini desserts, perfect for dolls, children, and anyone watching their waistline.

UNITED STATES BOTANIC GARDEN

Follow your nose. Or your eyes. Or your sense of humor. Or just follow the meandering paths around the amazing conservatory here. It's full of gardens to delight the senses and tickle the fancy with exotic, strange, rare, and beautiful plants from all over the world.

George Washington, Thomas Jefferson, and James Madison all envisioned a national botanic garden. Congress ultimately established it in 1820, the first greenhouse opened in 1842, and the current conservatory was completed in 1933. This national treasure, the delight of botany lovers big and small, is more magnificent than the founding fathers could have imagined.

Kids can see plants that dinosaurs might have munched on in the Garden Primeval (looking down at the pathway you'll spy dinosaurs' "footprints"). To learn how plants grow to become today's products, from fragrances to food, head to the Garden Court. See how bananas grow upside down from 20-foot stalks. Then check out the therapeutic uses of the specimens in Medicinal Plants.

MAKE THE MOST OF YOUR TIME If you'd like to chase a few butterflies, admire native plants, or simply linger outdoors longer, take time to explore the National Garden. Opened in 2006, it can be accessed from Independence Avenue or Maryland Avenue.

100 Maryland Ave. SW.
Metro: Federal Center Southwest

 Free

 Daily 10–5

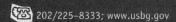 202/225–8333; www.usbg.gov

 2 and up

In World Deserts, cacti grow sharp spines (some of which look like fishhooks) as protection from grazing animals, though, of course, they aren't in any danger here. A sign explains how cacti expand and contract like accordions. Children may not be as enthused about orchids until they discover more about this diverse flowering family. For example, the beard orchid looks like it sprouted whiskers, and the mirror orchid attracts male wasps because its flowers resemble female wasps.

To really dig in, head to the Children's Garden (open spring–summer), where little green thumbed guests can try out gardening tools, meander through a tunnel made of bamboo, and hang out in a cottage the size of a playhouse. Push the hand pump and watch a fish spout water into a fountain.

If you like this sight, you may also like the United States National Arboretum (#8).

KEEP IN MIND Read the signs carefully. With the exception of the Children's Garden, kids should not touch any plants unless the staff specifically invites them to do so. Allow at least an hour to see what's in bloom when you visit and to plant some seeds of wisdom in your own little gardeners.

EATS FOR KIDS If you bring your own **picnic**, you're welcome to sit out on the terrace in the summer or at the **First Ladies Water Garden** (part of the National Garden). For ice cream and other foods, *see* eatery listings under the United States Capitol, the National Museum of the American Indian, the National Gallery of Art, and the National Air and Space Museum. On a pleasant day, bring your meal over to Bartholdi Park, across Independence Avenue from the Conservatory. Frédéric Auguste Bartholdi, designer of the huge historic fountain, is best known for designing the Statue of Liberty.

UNITED STATES CAPITOL

Throughout the Capitol, statues, paintings, and even the rooms themselves reveal much about the people and events that shaped our nation. The frieze around the rim of the Rotunda depicts 400 years of recognizable American history. Columbus's arrival, the California Gold Rush, and the Wright brothers' historic flight are all here. Eight immense oil paintings depict historical scenes, four from the Revolutionary War period. See if your child can find Pocahontas in the Rotunda. (Hint: She's in three places and doesn't resemble Disney's animated heroine.)

To tour the Capitol, you can book free advance passes through the website or obtain them by contacting your representative's or senator's office. You can also take a chance that same-day passes are available at the Capitol Visitor Center's information desks. For passes to the chambers of the House and Senate, you must go through your representative's or senator's office. If the House Chamber looks familiar to your child, you've probably let him or her stay up to watch the annual State of the Union speech. On the Senate side,

KEEP IN MIND

Keeping a secret is hard in Statuary Hall. Because of its perfectly elliptical ceiling, a slight whisper spoken on one side of the hall can be heard on the other. On tour, try it. If the room isn't too noisy, the trick may work.

MAKE THE MOST OF YOUR TIME
If you're taking the 50-minute guided tour, plan for at least another 30 minutes of waiting and going through security. To enhance your children's experience, talk about Congress's role in our government and the Capitol's place in history before you arrive. Then, during the tour, encourage them to move up front so they can see and hear better. Sometimes kids want to know how long it took to build the Capitol. The answer: 200 years and still building.

 East end of Mall.
Metro: Capitol South, Federal Triangle

 Free

 M–Sa 8:30–4:30; hrs subject to change

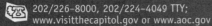 202/226–8000, 202/224–4049 TTY;
www.visitthecapitol.gov or www.aoc.gov

8 and up

look for the sixth desk from the right in the back row. Since 1968, whoever occupies the desk keeps the drawer filled with candy (sorry, no samples!).

Allow about two to three hours to tour the Capitol and its visitor center. Throughout the visitor center and National Statuary Hall, you'll find statues of people representing each state. Challenge younger kids to find statues of someone carrying a spear, a helmet, a book, and a baby. There's even a statue of a seven-year-old girl (Helen Keller). Tweens can look for statues of the person who invented television, a king, a physician, and a representative who said, "I cannot vote for war."

If you like this sight, you may also like seeing the other two big branches of government: the White House (#2) and the Supreme Court (1 1st St., NE, tel. 202/479–3030; www.supremecourt.gov).

EATS FOR KIDS Even though it's rare to find them here, the restaurant in the Center has enough seats in the **cafeteria** for every member of the House of Representative and all the Senators. The 550-seat venue serves basic American fare from 8:30 to 4. Sometimes, Senate bean soup is on the menu. This simple dish has been served in the exclusive Senate Dining Room every day for more than 100 years. You can try making your own using the recipe on the Senate's website (www.senate.gov).

UNITED STATES HOLOCAUST
MEMORIAL MUSEUM

Like the history it covers, the Holocaust Museum can be profoundly moving and emotionally complex, so you should first decide whether your children will be able to appreciate it. The recommended ages published by the museum are guidelines only. During the busy tourist season (March–August), the museum is often crowded, making it difficult to obtain tickets. The average visit is long, often two to three hours, and exhibits involve lots of reading. All that said, a trip can prove unforgettable for tweens or teens.

You don't need a pass for Remember the Children: Daniel's Story, an interactive exhibit that relates the history of the Holocaust from the perspective of a young boy growing up in Nazi Germany. Children follow events in Daniel's life. For example, they can see and touch his family's suitcases and clothing, and look into their ghetto apartment. At the end, they're invited to write about their thoughts and feelings. It's a helpful outlet. You can then gauge whether to proceed to the main exhibition.

This tells the story of millions of Jews, Gypsies, Polish Catholic civilians, Jehovah's Witnesses, homosexuals, political prisoners, and others killed by the Nazis between 1933

KEEP IN MIND Kids have shown they care and they will remember. More than 3,000 American schoolchildren put their feelings on porcelain for the Children's Tile Wall on the lower level. They painted flowers, peace signs, clasped hands, many versions of the word "hope," and more in this moving tribute.

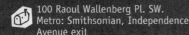
100 Raoul Wallenberg Pl. SW.
Metro: Smithsonian, Independence
Avenue exit

202/488–0400, 202/488–0406 TTY;
www.ushmm.org

Free; advance passes
required Mar–Aug, $1 fee
applies when ordering
online (tel. 800/400–9373;
www.ushmm.org/visit)

Daily 10–5:20

11 and up; Remember
the Children, 8 and up

and 1945. Striving to give a realistic first-person experience, the presentation is as extraordinary as the subject matter: On arrival, each visitor is issued an "identity card" containing biographical information on a real person from the Holocaust. As you move through the museum, you read sequential updates on your card—and, as you'd expect, the news isn't always good.

The museum recounts the Holocaust through documentary films, oral histories, and artifacts such as a freight car, like those used to transport Jews from Warsaw to the Treblinka death camp. Although there are four privacy walls to protect visitors from graphic images, they don't cover all that is horrific. After this powerful journey, the adjacent Hall of Remembrance provides space for quiet reflection.

If you like this sight, you may also like the National World War II Memorial, between the Lincoln Memorial (#48) and the Washington Monument (#6).

MAKE THE MOST OF YOUR TIME
To avoid long lines from March through August, order advance tickets through the website. Ideally, it might be best for you to visit the museum without your children initially to determine its appropriateness for your family. If that's not possible, consider going through Daniel's Story first.

EATS FOR KIDS
The **Museum Café** (tel. 202/488–6151), open 8:30–4:30, offers a variety of dishes, including matzoh-ball soup, kosher Asian-noodle salads, and even peanut butter and jelly sandwiches.

UNITED STATES NATIONAL ARBORETUM

8

How does your garden grow? This one grows with priceless, 200-year-old trees, herbs, aquatic plants, and 15,000 magnificent azaleas. The arboretum has two entrances: New York Avenue and R Street, off Bladensburg Road. Whichever you choose, your first stop should be the administration building, where speckled, orange koi fish flourish in the surrounding pool. Some koi, also called Japanese carp, are as long as a child's arm, others as little as a finger. For 50¢, you can buy pellets from dispensers that resemble gumball machines and feed the fish. Afterward, grab a map inside the visitor center. You'll need it. Almost 9 miles of winding roads cover 446 acres of botanical masterpieces.

Make sure you visit the National Bonsai & Penjing Museum. (In Japan artistic potted plants are bonsai and in China tray landscapes are called *penjing*.) These arts were depicted in paintings as early as the 6th century. The idea is simple: Just as you get your hair cut to achieve a desired look, so these trees are trimmed for a desired look, which may vary by species. The trees are worth "about as much as your children," according to the curator.

MAKE THE MOST OF YOUR TIME
You may drive, bike, walk, or do a little of each around the arboretum. If your kids bring their own wheels, there are racks for locking bicycles scattered around. Driving is slow—the speed limit is 20 mph and enforced—but you can park at each garden/museum within the arboretum. There's also a tram that runs on weekends and holidays, mid–April through mid–October ($4 adults, $2 children 4–16). The 40-minute ride may be good for older kids who are really into horticulture; however, it doesn't make stops, so it's not ideal for an intensive look at the gardens.

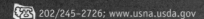 3501 New York Ave. NE

 Free

202/245-2726; www.usna.usda.gov

 Daily 8–5; National Bonsai & Penjing Museum daily 10–4

2 and up

Many have been nurtured for generations, and some were gifts to presidents. Your budding botanists can wander through outdoor rooms in search of the oldest trees, the smallest trees, or those with interesting trunks. Follow your nose to the National Herb Garden, where herbs from around the world are arranged. Kids can have fun sniffing out oregano, wild strawberries, licorice, English lavender, and ginger. Dozens of heritage roses also bloom here. Fruits, vegetables, and flowers thrive in the Youth Garden, planted by schoolchildren, who share what they grow with the homeless.

But plants aren't the only things jutting out from the earth. Twenty-two sandstone Corinthian columns that once stood at the east portico of the U.S. Capitol are set in a rectangle on a hill in a meadow.

If you like this sight, you may also like the Kenilworth National Aquatic Gardens (#50).

KEEP IN MIND
At the National Grove of State Trees, you can search for the official ones of all 50 states and the District of Columbia. Pick up a state tree list at the administration building. Don't look for markers on the ground; identification tags hang from branches.

EATS FOR KIDS When you're ready to feed your children, don't be tempted to pick the fruits, vegetables, or herbs, no matter how delicious they appear. (Think the Garden of Eden.) A **vendor** serving drinks and snacks comes sporadically on pleasant weekends, spring through fall. But your best bet is to pack your own food and dine under the state trees or at tables with umbrellas on the terrace next to where the koi fish swim. Just remind your kids not to feed the fish leftover crusts from sandwiches or even a carrot; they have a strict diet.

VIETNAM VETERANS MEMORIAL

Sometimes kids ask some serious questions about war and death after visiting this moving memorial to the more than 58,250 men and women who died in Vietnam. Sometimes children think they're all buried at the monument. They aren't, of course, but the slabs of black granite inscribed with the names of the dead are as somber, as powerful, and as evocative as any cemetery.

Known as "the Wall," the memorial is one of the most visited sites in Washington. Conceived by Jan Scruggs, a former infantry corporal who had served in Vietnam, these granite panels that reflect the sky, the trees, and the faces of those looking for names (and perhaps crying when they find them) were designed by Maya Ying Lin, a 21-year-old architectural student at Yale. The nontraditional war memorial was originally decried by some veterans, but with the addition of a flagpole just south of the Wall as well as Frederick Hart's statue of three soldiers, most critics were won over.

EATS FOR KIDS

Grab a hot dog or hamburger at a **food kiosk** behind the nearby Korean War Veterans Memorial.

MAKE THE MOST OF YOUR TIME Decode the symbols. Every name is preceded (on the West Wall) or followed (on the East Wall) by a symbol designating status. A diamond indicates "killed, body recovered." A small percentage of names have plus signs, indicating "killed: body not recovered." The remains of several hundred men have been found and identified, so the symbols next to their names were changed to diamonds. If a man returns alive, a circle, as a symbol of life, will be inscribed around the plus sign. Alas, there have not been any circles added.

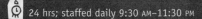

 Constitution Gardens, 22nd St. and Constitution Ave. NW.
Metro: Foggy Bottom

 Free

202/426–6841; www.nps.gov/vive

24 hrs; staffed daily 9:30 AM–11:30 PM

 9 and up

People's names appear on the Wall in the order of the date they died. To look up a name yourself, refer to the books posted at the entrance and exit of the memorial or ask at the white kiosk with the brown roof near the entrance. At the Wall, rangers and volunteers wearing yellow caps can look up names and supply you with graphite pencils and paper to make rubbings of them.

Thousands of offerings are left here each year. Although many people still leave flowers, remembrances have been evolving from personal objects, such as letters from soldiers and clothing they wore, to thank-you letters from school children.

If you like this sight, you may also like the World War II Memorial and the Korean War Memorial nearby. How does each memorial pay tribute to the soldiers who served? Encourage your child to talk with the park rangers at each site.

KEEP IN MIND Many people are surprised to learn that although 10,000 women served in Vietnam, only eight women's names are on the Wall. One of these is Mary Klinker. She was a nurse involved in Operation Baby Lift, a mission to bring Vietnamese orphans to the United States. Klinker's plane crashed in 1975.

WASHINGTON MONUMENT

Some kids say the Washington Monument looks like a giant pencil. Others think this 555' 5.9" obelisk (10 times as tall as its width at the base) punctuates the capital like a huge, partially buried exclamation point. Visible from nearly everywhere in the city, it's a landmark for visiting tourists and lost motorists alike and a beacon for anyone who yearns to shoot to the top and survey all of Washington below.

If you notice someone scaling the monument Spiderman-style or see scaffolding covering the building, that means it is still being repaired. This beloved structure closed on August 23, 2011, after a rare but powerful 5.8-magnitude earthquake hit 320 miles away in Bristol, Virginia. The quake sent tremors that rattled the mighty monument, leaving visible cracks and structural damage. Repair work is expected to last until the end of 2013.

When the monument reopens, lines will again snake around it. But they'll move quickly. (Ask impatient kids to count the flags surrounding the site.) Once inside, an elevator whizzes you to the top in 70 seconds, a trip that originally took about 12 minutes in a steam-powered elevator back in 1888 when the monument opened to visitors.

KEEP IN MIND A lot of people are curious about the color change about a third of the way up on the monument. It took more than 50 years to build this obelisk. Fund-raising began in 1833, and the cornerstone was laid in 1848; however, by 1854, construction had stopped and it didn't continue until after the Civil War. Although builders used marble from the same Maryland quarries, it was from a different stratum and of a slightly different shade. At its completion, the Washington Monument was the world's tallest structure. It's still the tallest in D.C.

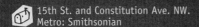
15th St. and Constitution Ave. NW.
Metro: Smithsonian

202/426 6841; www.nps.gov/
wamo/index.htm

Free; $1.50 fee applies for
advance tickets (tel. 877/444–
6777; www.recreation.gov)

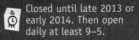
Closed until late 2013 or
early 2014. Then open
daily at least 9–5.

5 and up

Each of the four sides has two viewing stations, and every other station is equipped with a step. Gazing downward, small children may think Washington looks like Legoland. Older children may enjoy trying to spot famous landmarks. On a very clear day, you can see Shenandoah National Park to the west.

When you're ready to descend, go down one flight of stairs to the elevator. This level also houses a small bookshop that carries a modest selection of children's books about Washington the place and Washington the man. Having now been in the monument, take another good look up at it from the ground. Unlike a pencil lead (made of graphite), the monument is topped with a 7½-pound piece of aluminum, a very expensive metal in 1884, when the monument was completed.

If you like this sight, you may also like George Washington's home, Mount Vernon (#44).

EATS FOR KIDS

You can't take anything up with you, but a **refreshment stand** sells ice cream in summer, hot chocolate in winter, and sandwiches year-round. For some down-to-earth good food, see the restaurants listed for the United States Holocaust Memorial Museum and National Museum of American History.

MAKE THE MOST OF YOUR TIME

Judging by the crowds, it seems there are as many people who want to look down on the Washington action literally as there are those who look down on it figuratively. If the monument is still closed or you don't want to wait in line, head to Washington National Cathedral's Pilgrim Observation Gallery (*see* #5) or the Old Post Office (100 Pennsylvania Ave., at 12th St. NW, tel. 202/606–8691). The Newseum (*see* #24) is another option for beautiful views of the U.S. Capitol, National Gallery of Art, and the National Mall.

WASHINGTON NATIONAL CATHEDRAL

Boys and girls go Gothic at the world's sixth-largest cathedral. Like its 14th-century counterparts, the National Cathedral (officially Washington's Cathedral Church of St. Peter and St. Paul) has flying buttresses and 100-foot vaulted ceilings that were built stone by stone. Fanciful gargoyles adorn the outside of the building. The Cathedral is Episcopalian, but it's the site of ecumenical and interfaith services.

You can pick up a printed family guide at the welcome desk just inside the main entrance. A stained-glass window with an encapsulated moon rock celebrates the *Apollo 11* flight, and the flags and seals of all 50 states are on display. Kids also like counting the pennies in the floor of Lincoln Bay, and some visitors leave food for the poor at the feet of the president for whom it was named. A charming children's chapel tantalizes the imagination with depictions of real and imaginary animals. Kneelers depict the story of Noah's ark. If you have time to spare, see how far you get counting the pieces of stained glass that make up the West Rose window. There are more than 10,500!

MAKE THE MOST OF YOUR TIME

Although the cathedral is a cool place for kids, it's still a house of worship. So encourage them to be as quiet as, well, church mice, in the main sanctuary and chapels. If they need to let off steam, the Bishop's Garden is ideal for hide-and-seek.

EATS FOR KIDS The only place to eat on the cathedral grounds is the **Cathedral Store** (tel. 202/537–6267), which has sandwiches, snacks, and tempting fudge. The cathedral is surrounded by gardens that are great for a picnic, however. A few blocks north you can find **Cactus Cantina** (3300 Wisconsin Ave. NW, tel. 202/686–7222), a lively Mexican restaurant where President George W. Bush and Laura Bush dined; **Cafe Deluxe** (3228 Wisconsin Ave. NW, tel. 202/686–2233), which includes a three-vegetable entrée among its children's offerings; and **2 Amys** (3715 Macomb St., tel. 202/885–5700), known as the best gourmet pizza place in the city.

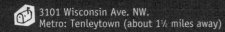 3101 Wisconsin Ave. NW.
Metro: Tenleytown (about 1½ miles away)

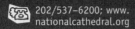 202/537-6200; www.
nationalcathedral.org

 $10 donation
suggested

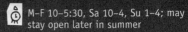 M–F 10–5:30, Sa 10–4, Su 1–4; may
stay open later in summer

 4 and up

Hidden from view on the south side of the Cathedral, the English-style Bishop's Garden looks like the setting of the classic children's book *The Secret Garden* by Frances Hodgson Burnett. Boxwoods, ivy, tea roses, yew trees, and an assortment of arches, bas-reliefs, and stonework from European ruins provide a counterpoint to the cathedral's towers.

Upwardly mobile boys and girls can ascend the 333 steps (many on a spiral staircase) to the top of the cathedral's central tower. The climb is usually only open a few times per year. If you're looking for a bird's-eye view, visit the Pilgrim Observation Gallery. It's open almost every day. From the gallery, you can see the whole city of Washington—and even the Blue Ridge Mountains on a clear day. Test your observation skills and see how many Washington landmarks you spy through the windows.

If you like this sight, you may also like the United States Capitol (#10).

KEEP IN MIND At the east side of St. Peter's tower, almost at the top, is a stone grotesque of Darth Vader. A 13-year-old boy suggested the carving in a contest to design a decorative sculpture for the cathedral. Bring binoculars. They make Vader—and a lot of the other gargoyles—easier to spot.

WASHINGTON NATIONALS

4

Baseball fans have much to cheer about in D.C. Baseball returned to the District in 2005 after a 33-year break, a brand new stadium (Nationals Park) was built in 2008, and the team turned the whole town red after winning its division in 2012.

Despite its long hiatus, professional baseball enjoys a long and rich history in our nation's capital that extends back to the late 19th century. The very first pro team in D.C. was the Olympic Baseball Club of Washington in 1871; another called Capital Cities from the League of Colored Baseball Clubs arrived in 1887. The game has a huge African American following here, and from the late 1930s through World War II, the Homestead Grays—perhaps the greatest Negro League team ever—ran the bases in the District.

The Nationals, unofficially nicknamed the Nats, are represented by a group of young adults called the Nat Pack that revs up the crowd and helps give away T-shirts, pizzas, magnets, and other goodies. On Sunday after the game, kids take to the field for the Diamond dash. The team's mascot, named Screech, predictably is an eagle, but some folks think he looks more like a chicken!

KEEP IN MIND Washington, D.C., is also a mecca for youth soccer. If your kids get a kick out of this international sport, consider cheering on the D.C. United Soccer team (202/587–5000; www.dcunited.com), which plays at nearby RFK Stadium. One of 19 MLS (Major League Soccer) teams in the country, D.C. United has won more major national and international championships than any other U.S. team in history. Plays are called in both English and Spanish. Arrive early on weekends to participate in free speed kicks, dribbling contests, and other activities just for kids outside the stadium.

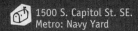
1500 S. Capitol St. SE.
Metro: Navy Yard

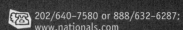
202/640–7580 or 888/632–6287;
www.nationals.com

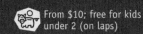
From $10; free for kids
under 2 (on laps)

Early Apr–Oct. Gates open
1½ hrs before game time

4 and up

If your little ones are more interested in Screech than in the game itself, a kid zone to the left of the entrance combines playground equipment geared toward three- to eight-year-olds with activities for older siblings, including a video arcade and cages for batting and pitching. Kids who really love Screech can make their own through the on-site Build-A-Bear franchise.

Be sure to be in your seats for the fourth inning, when 10-foot-tall caricatures of the presidents on Mount Rushmore take to the field in the middle of the inning. Who will win? Washington, Jefferson, Lincoln, or Teddy Roosevelt? Find out at the game.

If you like this sight, you may also enjoy another local team, the Minor League's Bowie Baysox Baseball (Prince George's Stadium, 4101 Crain Hwy, Bowie, MD, tel. 301/805–6000 or 301/464–4865; www.baysox.com).

MAKE THE MOST OF YOUR TIME

If your kids need to burn some excess energy before or after the game, check out Diamond Teague Park (100 Potomac Ave., SE; www.capitolriverfront.org) across from the stadium. There's a wading pool, tables and chairs, and plenty of room for a game of tag.

EATS FOR KIDS On-site you can munch on classic ballpark fare such as hot dogs, chicken tenders, and peanuts, or order kosher, Chinese, and Chesapeake Bay cuisine. Food is cheaper across the street at **Fairgrounds** (1299 Half St. SE, 201/244–0592), but pitching games and beanbag tosses for tots may make it hard to leave. The eatery (formerly known as Bullpen) is open only on game days.

WHEATON REGIONAL PARK

All aboard! A little red replica of an 1863 train chugs along on 10-minute tours through the woods at this park located within 10 miles of D.C. But there's more for children here than just choo-choo rides.

Youngsters can go for a spin on a carousel, ride a life-size statue of a camel, or zip down banana-yellow slides at the playground, which was renovated in 2012. There are lots of climbing options, too—from walls and webs to a mound that can make even a toddler feel like king of the hill.

Facilities for sports lovers include hiking trails, an ice rink, tennis courts, a fishing pond, baseball fields, basketball courts and horse stables (301/622–2424; www. wheatonparkstables.com). The Brookside Nature Center offers dozens of free and low-cost nature programs throughout the year (hikes, puppet shows, workshops, and summer camps among them). Even without a special program, though, the nature center is a

EATS FOR KIDS

Picnic tables are scattered throughout the park. **Westfield Wheaton** shopping mall (11160 Viers Mill Rd., tel. 301/942–3200; www.westfield.com/wheaton), about 3 miles away, has a **food court**.

MAKE THE MOST OF YOUR TIME

If you're closer to the Potomac, you may prefer the 528-acre Cabin John Regional Park (7400 Tuckerman La., Rockville, MD, tel. 301/299–0024). Youngsters can swing, slide, and climb on playground equipment or watch the Bethesda Big Train baseball team (tel. 301/983–1006; www. bigtrain.org) play in a summer league there. Facilities also include a train replica that takes children through the forest and alongside the playground, where kids often wave to the train passengers. Feed trash to "Porky," the talking pig near the station.

2000 Shorefield Rd., Wheaton, MD; 1400 Glenallan Ave., Brookside Nature Center; 1800 Glenallan Ave., Brookside Gardens

 301/495-2595, 301/962-1480 nature center, 301/962-1400 gardens; www.montgomeryparks.org, www.brooksidenature.org, www.brooksidegardens.org

 Free; some attractions charge

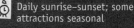 Daily sunrise-sunset; some attractions seasonal

 6 months and up

fun place to visit. Kids can check out live snakes, fish, and turtles; play nature games on the computer; and assemble puzzles.

Next to the nature center is Brookside Gardens, where formal seasonal displays of bulbs, annuals, and perennials and a sprawling azalea garden flourish outside, and seasonal displays and exotic tropicals blossom inside. Butterflies from North America and Costa Rica flutter freely indoors at the Wings of Fancy exhibit from early May through mid-September. The garden's annual children's day (held on the third or fourth Saturday in September) features activities, crafts, and games.

If you like this sight, you may also like the United States National Arboretum (#8).

KEEP IN MIND You won't see Santa or a menorah at Brookside's seasonal Garden of Lights, but you will see bears, owls, squirrels, cherry trees, and black-eyed Susans—all lit up brighter than stars to enchant children of all ages and all faiths. Many local families make this light show a holiday tradition. For a decent parking space on weekends, be sure to arrive early.

WHITE HOUSE

It's amazing that the country's most renowned residence—the historic house President Eisenhower once called "a living story of past pioneering, struggles, wars, innovations, and a growing America"—remains open to visitors. Getting in, however, does take advance planning because you must make tour arrangements through a member of Congress. Tours are scheduled on a first-come, first-served basis. You'll be asked for the names, birth dates, and Social Security numbers of everyone in your group. To visit in January, a month might be sufficient notice, but to visit in spring or summer you will need to request possible dates approximately six months in advance.

Self-guided tours last about 20–25 minutes—which is about the same amount of time you'll need to go through security. Everyone 18 years of older must present a government-issued photo ID.

KEEP IN MIND The White House Visitor Center (1450 Pennsylvania Ave. NW, tel. 202/208–1631) is undergoing renovations and not slated to reopen until the fall of 2013. In the interim, a small trailer with a concession stand, restrooms, and water fountains serves as a temporary welcome center. You'll find it near the Ellipse Visitor Pavilion, just west of the intersection of 15th and E streets, NW. Official White House merchandise is on sale nearby at Decatur House (1610 H St. NW, tel. 202/218–4338) on weekdays.

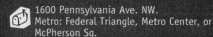 1600 Pennsylvania Ave. NW.
Metro: Federal Triangle, Metro Center, or
McPherson Sq.

 Free

 T–Sa 7:30–11 (groups only; tours
may be canceled without notice);
Visitor center daily 7:30–4

 202/456-7041 or 202/208–1631;
www.whitehouse.gov, www.nps.gov/whho

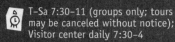 5 and up

You'll walk through the East Room (where Teddy Roosevelt allowed his children to ride a pony and where the Jonas Brothers surprised Barack Obama's girls), the State Dining Room (where Bill Clinton's daughter, Chelsea, hosted pizza parties), plus rooms named after the colors of the walls and furnishings (picture the Green Room, the Blue Room, and the Red Room, a favorite of first ladies).

Many children naturally hope to the see the president in person, or at least catch a glimpse of a presidential pet. If yours are disappointed that they didn't get a chance to chat with the Commander in Chief (perhaps they feel obliged to tell him that it's time to change the color scheme of the house), they may send an email to president@whitehouse.gov or pen a letter and send it to him via "snail mail." The First Family even has its own zip code: 20500.

If you like this sight, you may also like the U.S. Capitol (#10).

MAKE THE MOST OF YOUR TIME

Are you ready to roll? Kids have been rolling eggs on the White House lawn every Easter Monday since the 1800s. Unlike previous generations, though, you can't just show up that morning and expect to participate. You'll need luck or connections. Nevertheless, it's worth a try to be able to say that your children played at the president's house!

EATS FOR KIDS Healthy eaters inspired by the veggies in the First Lady's garden can get organic treats near the White House from the **FARMFRESH** market at Lafayette Park (810 Vermont Ave. NW, between H St. NW and I St. NW, tel. 202/362–8889) from 11 to 2:30 on Friday, May through October. At **Old Ebbitt Grill** (675 15th St. NW, tel. 202/347–4800), a Washington tradition since 1856, parents like the homemade pasta, while children opt for kids' menu choices including grilled cheese and hot dogs.

WOLF TRAP NATIONAL PARK
FOR THE PERFORMING ARTS

Over a stream and through the woods, you can find a clearing with benches and a stage where Wolf Trap and the National Park Service present Theatre-in-the-Woods for at least seven weeks every summer. Though Wolf Trap is most often associated with adult concerts, as many as 800 people per show come here to see professional children's performers, such as jugglers, musicians, clowns, storytellers, and puppeteers.

Special events are another draw. On the first Saturday in December, for instance, families with children of all ages gather at Wolf Trap for the annual Holiday Sing-A-Long to celebrate the songs of both Christmas and Hanukkah. The only admission requested for this free event is a new toy for Toys for Tots.

Any time of year, romping through the park is encouraged. Children (and parents) roll down the grassy hill and picnic in the meadow under shady trees. Because Wolf Trap is a national park, rangers are available to answer questions about flora and fauna and hand

MAKE THE MOST OF YOUR TIME

Theatre-in-the-Woods shows often sell out. So if your child really wants to see a certain performance— or you really want to introduce your child to a certain art form (opera, for example)— pick up tickets in advance at the Filene Center.

KEEP IN MIND If you want to come back and see a performance at night, you'll have more than 200 to choose from between the outdoor 7,000-seat Filene Center and the indoor 380-seat Barns at Wolf Trap. If you choose to bring your children to the outdoor arena, the lawn is a wonderful place for families to lounge and picnic on blankets.

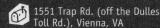 
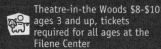
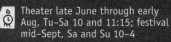

out activity booklets. Sometimes, they also give impromptu nature tours after performances in the woods. Rangers may point out Virginia's state tree (the dogwood) and its state bird (the cardinal), or explain how the bark and roots of the sassafras tree were used not only to make perfume, soap, and medicine, but also to flavor root beer.

Wondering why this place is called Wolf Trap? During Colonial times, when the area was farmland, the farmers who considered wolves a danger to livestock would reward anyone who trapped the creatures. There haven't been wolves here for ages, but you may spot deer, foxes, or groundhogs.

If you like this sight, you may also like Glen Echo Park (#55).

EATS FOR KIDS No food or drink (except water) is permitted in the theater because bees and animals might want to join you for lunch. If you bring food on-site, you'll have to keep it securely wrapped in a squirrel-proof container (think hard plastic instead of paper) during the show. For evening performances at Wolf Trap, whether you bring your own food or buy from their **vendors**, you're welcome to stretch out on the lawn.

CLASSIC GAMES

"I SEE SOMETHING YOU DON'T SEE AND IT IS BLUE." Stuck for a way to get your youngsters to settle down in a museum? Sit them on a bench in the middle of a room and play this vintage favorite. The leader gives just one clue—the color—and everybody guesses away.

"I'M GOING TO THE GROCERY STORE . . ." The first player begins, "I'm going to the grocery store and I'm going to buy . . .," finishing the sentence with the name of an object found in grocery stores that begins with the letter "A." The second player repeats what the first player has said, and adds the name of another item that starts with "B." The third player repeats everything that has been said so far and adds something that begins with "C," and so on through the alphabet. Anyone who skips or misremembers an item is out (or decide up front that you'll give hints to all who need 'em). You can modify the theme depending on where you're going that day, as "I'm going to X and I'm going to see . . ."

FAMILY ARK Noah had his ark—here's your chance to build your own. It's easy: Just start naming animals and work your way through the alphabet, from antelope to zebra.

PLAY WHILE YOU WAIT

NOT THE GOOFY GAME Have one child name a category. (Some ideas: first names, last names, animals, countries, friends, feelings, foods, hot or cold things, clothing.) Then take turns naming things that fall into it. You're out if you name something that doesn't belong in the category—or if you can't think of another item to add. When only one person remains, start again. Choose categories depending on where you're going or where you've been—historic topics if you've seen a historic sight, animal topics before or after the zoo, upside-down things if you've been to the circus, and so on. Make the game harder by choosing category items in A-B-C order.

DRUTHERS How do your kids really feel about things? Just ask. "Would you rather eat worms or hamburgers? Hamburgers or candy?" Choose serious and silly topics—and have fun!

BUILD A STORY "Once upon a time there lived . . ." Finish the sentence and ask the rest of your family, one at a time, to add another sentence or two. If you can, record the narrative so you can enjoy your creation again and again.

GOOD TIMES GALORE

WIGGLE & GIGGLE Give your kids a chance to stick out their tongues at you. Start by making a face, then have the next person imitate you and add a gesture of his own—snapping fingers, winking, clapping, sneezing, or the like. The next person mimics the first two and adds a third gesture, and so on.

JUNIOR OPERA During a designated period of time, have your kids sing everything they want to say.

THE QUIET GAME Need a good giggle—or a moment of calm to figure out your route? The driver sets a time limit and everybody must be silent. The last person to make a sound wins.

MANY THANKS

This book is dedicated with appreciation to the museum guides, naturalists, docents, and volunteers who make Washington such an enriching environment for children. On a personal note, for helping me to witness Washington's wonders through the eyes of children, I am grateful to my sons, Norman and Tim, and their nine cousins, Anastasia, Brady, Diana, Eddie, Erin, Kate, Mary, Matthew, and Owens.

—Kathryn McKay